STEAMBOATS
OF
GLOUCESTER
AND THE
NORTH SHORE

STEAMBOATS
OF
GLOUCESTER
AND THE
NORTH SHORE

JOHN LESTER SUTHERLAND

CHARLESTON   LONDON

the
History
PRESS

Published by The History Press
18 Percy Street
Charleston, SC 29403
866.223.5778
www.historypress.net

Manufactured in the United Kingdom   ˜

ISBN: 1-59629-000-5

Library of Congress CIP data applied for.

CONTENTS

Dedicated to William John Sutherland 1886-1970. *J.L. Sutherland*.

PREFACE

At the onset, I want to impress upon the reader, that in composing this work, it is not my intent for it to be some kind of biography of my father. The reader will notice many referrals to his work and career, as well as the persons he worked with, if only to show that he and others were part of the greater picture in the active structure of the working harbor.

It is primarily my intent to supplement what has already appeared in print and to extend the range of the supporting marine activity around Gloucester Harbor from 1869 to the end of 1947.

Therefore, in the interest of brevity, it is imperative to divide the subject into two definitive areas. It is not about the great fishing schooners, nor the fishing industry as a whole. Volumes have been written about that particular aspect of Gloucester's history. Conversely, the thread of this presentation is devoted to the lesser-known working vessels, and as far as practicable, the persons and owners that labored in their daily routine, which had a somewhat diminished impact on the everyday workings of the city.

The first part involves the passenger and freight lines and services from 1869 until the last scheduled sailing of the S.S. *Myrtle II* in 1931. (Sprinkled throughout are items that may be of interest, such as the *Portland* disaster and the grounding of the *Rio Branco*.) The second part has to do with the workboats—tugs, water boats, and ferries—again, naming where possible, their crews and owners. Many illustrations show the wide variety of activities these boats were involved in.

This essay is not intended to infringe upon the historical efforts of the many dedicated members of the Gloucester Archives Committee, who published in 2002, their most enlightening publication, the *Historical Time-Line* edition that encompassed the years 1000–1999. There are gaps in the history of Gloucester harbor that need attention; perhaps this will suffice. Other authors' works will be referred to from time to time, and credits are appropriately entered in the appendix.

This literary production appears only to bring to light a somewhat neglected aspect of the cameo players in Gloucester harbor from about 1869 to 1947. It is my hope that the reading of this historical matter will be received as a postscript to the works of the past.

J.L. Sutherland

INTRODUCTION

When I was a kid, 70 and more years ago, most everything that was big and powerful was run by a coal-fired steam engine—no gasoline or oil, just harnessing the expansive potential of boiling water. Steam drove passenger liners and freighters across oceans, river boats up and down the Mississippi and the Essex, ferries and tugboats in and out of harbors, railroad locomotives hauling trains across the land, steam shovels and steamrollers and pile drivers building schools and skyscrapers, and for a few years it even powered very fast and almost silent automobiles.

In many ways for the worse, we outlived hot water and now rely on the world's diminishing reserves of oil for power—and on the memories of the fast-diminishing breed of steamboat men like John Lester (Let) Sutherland of Gloucester to tell us how it was in those last years of the era when the world's greatest fishing port thrived on wind at sea and steam along the coast.

I've known Let for 40 years, and he's the right stuff. His Pa came here from Scotland and climbed up through the hawse pipe, as they used to say, to be oiler and second engineer on the gull-white Boston–Gloucester steamship *Cape Ann*, the handsomest passenger vessel on the Atlantic coast, and after that he was a Gloucester towboat engineer.

And it was in those sunset years of the steam harbor tugs that the young Sutherland brothers followed their Dad through the figurative hawse pipe and learned the ways and the nigh forgotten technology of the steam-powered workhorse that has chugged off, almost to the gunwales in the water, and into the lore of the Gloucester maritime mystique as nostalgically as the patched wings of the sea-worn fishing schooners these jaunty stalwarts once towed, with throaty chugs amidst puffs of smoke and steam, from wharf to open Atlantic on a windless day.

A former plainspoken city councilor, coastal warden, and man of all work, our author talks like a writer and writes like a talker—the best of both, and both are here. He hadn't a book in mind when he began gathering memories and photographs and researching vessels and tugs and events and disasters and family and friends and old-time characters and stories and jokes and local lore galore with that sardonic, low-key, self-deprecating humor of his.

Nope, just wanted some recollections to hand on to his children and grandchildren. But when he showed me what he had, I showed it to my publisher, Kirsty Sutton of the up-and-coming History Press, and with a flick of her computer, Let became an author, as unforgettable as he is uneditable.

A few surprises, oh yes. Sutherland the master shipmodeller, whose brilliant rendition of the magical S.S. *Cape Ann* in Gloucester's Sawyer Free Library he conceived without builder's plans (for there are none) but from photographs.

And Sutherland the boatbuilder himself, who years ago, as he tells it here, transmogrified a beached-out old wreck into his *Sawdust Sally*, a wee steam-powered, canopied little yacht of an age gone by. He writes pleasantly enough of the festive day he chugged her by our house on the harbor shore of Eastern Point. When abreast of us, becalmed in our sailboat, he reached for his steam whistle cord and gave us a long blast that echoed around the harbor. That said, *Sally* drifted steamless to a stop.

But that's not her skipper's way. Read on.

Joseph E. Garland

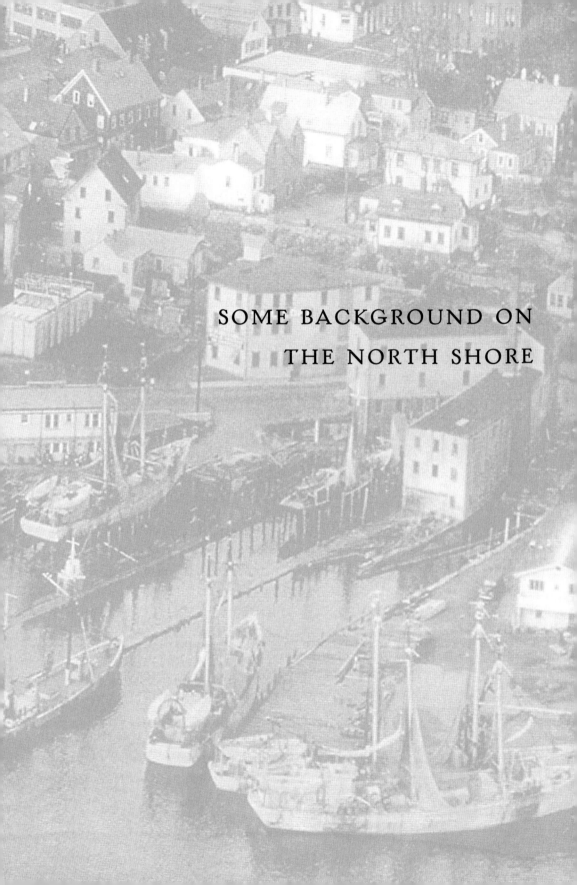

SOME BACKGROUND ON
THE NORTH SHORE

1

The time has arrived to give a methodical review of the supporting cast of vessels that, for the most part, have been neglected and that carried on their tasks in making this harbor a nearly complete entity in itself. The historic fishing industry of Gloucester could never exist without the wealth of tugs, ferries, gill-netters, water boats, seiners, and net establishments. There were sail lofts, dory builders, rope makers, grocers, and ship chandlers, among others, that contributed immensely to the well being of the fishing industry. This city's history is steeped in a tradition of men with courage to wrest a living from the sea. The general public, far removed from Gloucester, have only a passing knowledge of the everyday dangers the fishermen face, now as in the past, to make this port the greatest fishing port in the United States.

Some of our more fortunate men challenged the sea for many years, and survived the hardships endured. Thousands of others did not. Over the years, families and friends meet with dignitaries of the city at the fishermen's monument to pay homage to the lost souls, past and present that did not return to their home port.

The so-called "day boats," the local trappers, and mackerel seiners also contributed greatly to the ever-expanding economics of this city. Inshore fisheries were important. Gill-netters were, by far, the most active in the fresh fish business. Individually, their comings and goings are not nearly as exciting as the great sailing fishermen out of Gloucester. In the interest of brevity, I shall only touch upon the activities of the gill-netters with which I am most familiar.

It may be of interest to some that in the year I was born, 1922, the list of gill-netters recorded in the *Gloucester Daily Times* were *Orion, Enterprise, N. Bruce, Evelyn, Eliza C. Riggs, Julia May, Sunflower, Sawyer, Quoddy, C.A. Mister, Joanna, Ethel, Nirvinia,* and the *Robert and Edwin.* When I was between 12 and 14 years old, after school was out,

The placing of wreaths at the Fishermen's Statue, Gloucester, during the Annual Fishermen's Memorial Service. *Master Mariners Yearbook*.

the boats that I reeled nets for were many: the three *Naomi Bruces*, *Elizabeth and James*, *Enterprise*, *Lucrecia*, *Edna Fae*, *Lois T.*, *Mary A.*, *Aliburton*, *Austin W.*, *Polly T.*, *Jackie B.*, *Idle Hour*, and the *Agnes and Myrnie*. The going rate at that time was 25¢ a box, which was enough money to go to the Union Hill Theater on Saturday with some left over money for popcorn.

A TEMPERAMENTAL SEA

As in the far past, and as in recent years, the roll of missing vessels and men ever increases. Two examples of missing vessels and their crews come to mind from when I was a lad. I knew most of these men, and the effect it had on their families was devastating.

First, I should touch briefly on the ill-fated vessel the *Virginia and Joan II*. It was on November 10, 1936, that she was lost with all hands in Ipswich Bay while returning to port from a day of gill-netting on the ridge, near the Isles of Shoals, off New Hampshire. There was little or no warning that the weather would turn nasty, with winds reaching 60 to 70 m.p.h. The *Virginia and Joan II*, commissioned by Roland Wonson, was launched in Kennebunkport on June 3, 1934. Her particulars were as follows: length 55 feet, breadth 13.5 feet, and a 5-foot draft. It should be noted here that it was built with an open cock-pit–style aft. It was powered with an Atlas diesel (previously, a Cooper-Bessemer). The vessel was fishing the usual number of boxes of nets (28) and hauling the same number, far too many for that type of vessel, especially in the fall and winter months. It was voiced at the time that with 28 boxes of wet nets and several thousand pounds of pollack aboard, the scuppers must have been in the water. A good sea in that situation could only spell disaster.

The crew that day was Captain Austin Wonson (25 years old); C. Earl Gerring, engineer (30); Harold W. "Connie" Fairweather, the cook (36); Richard Frost (25); James "Jimmy" Jacobs (38); and Fredric Thompson, the captain's uncle and a passenger for the day (48).

Elliott Dagle, a shore hand for the boat, was to go out that day, but the captain couldn't raise him. It saved his life. Fairweather planned to quit the boat the next day to ship with his brother on the *Ethyl Huff*. Charles Martell quit the previous week to captain the gill-netter *Catherine*.

Fate plays out its hand, harshness to some, good luck to others. Some days later, the *Edna Fae* was hauling her nets in the bay, when Captain Hercules "Herkey" Ryan noticed what appeared to be a body in a lifejacket floating off the bow. The men gaffed it, and it was identified as the body of Harold Fairweather. Of the six aboard the ill-fated *Virginia and Joan II*, it was the only body recovered.

Another tragic ending occurred with *Austin W.* In 1938, Roland R. Wonson had a 66-foot vessel built in Kennebunkport, and he named it after his son, Austin W. It was ironic that this vessel, in later years, was also lost, with all hands, while fishing out of New York. It was assumed that the vessel was heading for home in a cold nor'wester and that she most probably "iced" up and capsized. No trace of the vessel or crew was ever found. In hindsight, with icing conditions prevailing, the prudent course of action would have been to head offshore and lay to in the Gulf Stream until the wind subsided. It would have delayed, by a day or so, their arrival at the Fulton Fish Market Pier, but perhaps lives could have been saved. In any case, as there were no survivors, what actually happened is a matter of conjecture.

The following event, happily, did not end with any loss of life. No article about gill-netting would be complete without mentioning the old 65-foot gill-netter *Lucrecia*. To say that this vessel had some age on her is an understatement. This vessel was built in 1898 for Gloucester's Salvatore Niscastro. It was amusingly said that near the end of her long career, the owners must have pumped out the equivalent of Gloucester harbor every day. This vessel was a gill-netter for most of her career, but the last years of her long life, she fished as an inshore dragger.

While the story of her ending may or may not be the truth, it is still a good yarn. Word was that her end came one day out in Ipswich Bay while fishing for whiting, a silvery fish in great demand. Her crew was hoisting a particularly large bag of fish over the rail, and not seeing the bag clear the rail, the skipper told the winch man to take another turn on the capstan head, for he thought the fish tackle was slipping a bit. The hand informed him that the winch was doing the job, as indeed it was.

Trouble was that no one noticed that the rigging was going slack until it was too late, and the mast itself was easing out through the vessel's bottom. Instead of the bag coming aboard, a law of physics was set in motion—you know, action, reaction, that sort of thing.

It wasn't long before the crew realized that they were in heap of trouble, and into the dory they went. Fact remains, the crew was picked up by a passing vessel.

The *Enterprise* was another old-timer, 61 feet long and built in 1904 in Fall River, Massachusetts, for Kale Tysver of Gloucester. It was said that she was steam powered at one time, and her old boiler was deposited under the wharf just ahead of where she moored. Kale Tysver was the captain. The description of this particular vessel, attributed to a friend of mine, a well-known East Gloucester fisherman and "wag" by the name of Captain Bill Sibley, was "three decks–no bottom." Last I heard of her was that she was sold down Cape Cod way.

Finally, it was on July 11, 1925, when the gill-netter *Anna T* was stranded on the rocks at the mouth of the Annisquam River in Gloucester. Captain Albert Arnold and his partner Philip Beaudine owned the vessel. Captain Gerry Shoares had borrowed the gill-netter to haul his gear in the bay, as his craft was on the ways being painted. For some reason, on her return trip, the *Anna T* lost power and took bottom on the bar at the river's entrance and drifted onto the rocks off of what is known as Annisquam. It was a total loss, but with no loss of life.

Captain Shoares had a new vessel built to replace the loss, and Captain Arnold and his partner named the new craft the *Phylis A* after Arnold's daughter. After having been nearly re-built over the years, she is still afloat. During her career, three Arnolds captained her: Albert, the original owner, and sons Alvin (the eldest) and Richard (the final captain). The

Gill-netters from Michigan in 1910. *Courtesy of Captain Richard E. Arnold.*

A second look at gill-netters from Michigan in 1910. *Courtesy of Captain Richard E. Arnold.*

vessel is now in Kennebunkport, Maine, in a museum not far from the place of her birth. For a while, I was the engineer aboard her.

As Richard and I were reminiscing, the subject came up about the first gill-netters in Gloucester. He gave me a bit of history. His photos show that the first boats that worked here were five 35- to 40-footers. Word was that in 1910, these men and boats came from the state of Michigan via the Great Lakes. His brother Alvin said that the trip took them through the Erie Canal, down the Hudson River, and east to Gloucester.

As the photos show, it must have been quite a trip. The travelers had been told to relay back to the people left behind, whether one could make a decent living here. The crews got to work right away. After only a week or so of fishing, they wired back that the fishing was out of this world, and that a lot of money could indeed be made here. Within days, back in Michigan, some of the owners packed up their belongings, put their boats on rail flat cars, and made the trip.

The gill-netters from Michigan soon found that their boats were wholly inadequate for the rigors of the North Atlantic, and soon the modern fleet, as we knew them a few years ago, came into being. These hardy souls were instrumental in making Gloucester the fishing capital of the world.

Burnham Brothers Railway in 1940. *Gloucester Maritime Heritage Center.*

WATERFRONT INDUSTRIES

Now, to get to the other industries that was instrumental in the welfare of the fleet and other so-called small insignificant vessels of the harbor. A good place as any to start is in Vincent Cove, where all manner of vessels, tugs, and lighters were built. Here, Tom Irving and John Bishop were the master shipbuilders. Joe Call's spar yard, close by, supplied the many masts and booms that propelled the sail-powered vessels.

The Cape Ann Anchor Works was nearby. All vessels had two anchors, plus two smaller tub trawl anchors for each of their dories. Vessels were also built and launched at Pavilion Beach, some smaller ones on Five Pound Island. There were two ropewalks in the city that, with their intricate weaving of the anchor ropes, or cables, and tub trawl lines, were kept busy. There were literally miles upon miles of manila (ropes), sheets, halyards, downhauls, and dory tackles, which were necessary to operate the sailing vessels and work boats. Block shops and oar makers (called ship chandlers) were in great demand.

Several rigging lofts were scattered around the waterfront. Sail lofts worked 12 hours or more a day, depending upon the emergency, providing work for hundreds of men. In summer, myriad windows gave light as well as air. In the winter months, when heat was needed, great pot-bellied stoves were hung by chain from the rafters to provide an unobstructed working floor. Care was taken to prevent fires, for if one got started, it created peril for not only that business, but the entire city proper as well.

A 1946 receipt from Gorton-Pew Fisheries Company, Ltd., of Gloucester. *J.L. Sutherland.*

A receipt from Parkhurst Marine Railway of Gloucester. *J.L. Sutherland.*

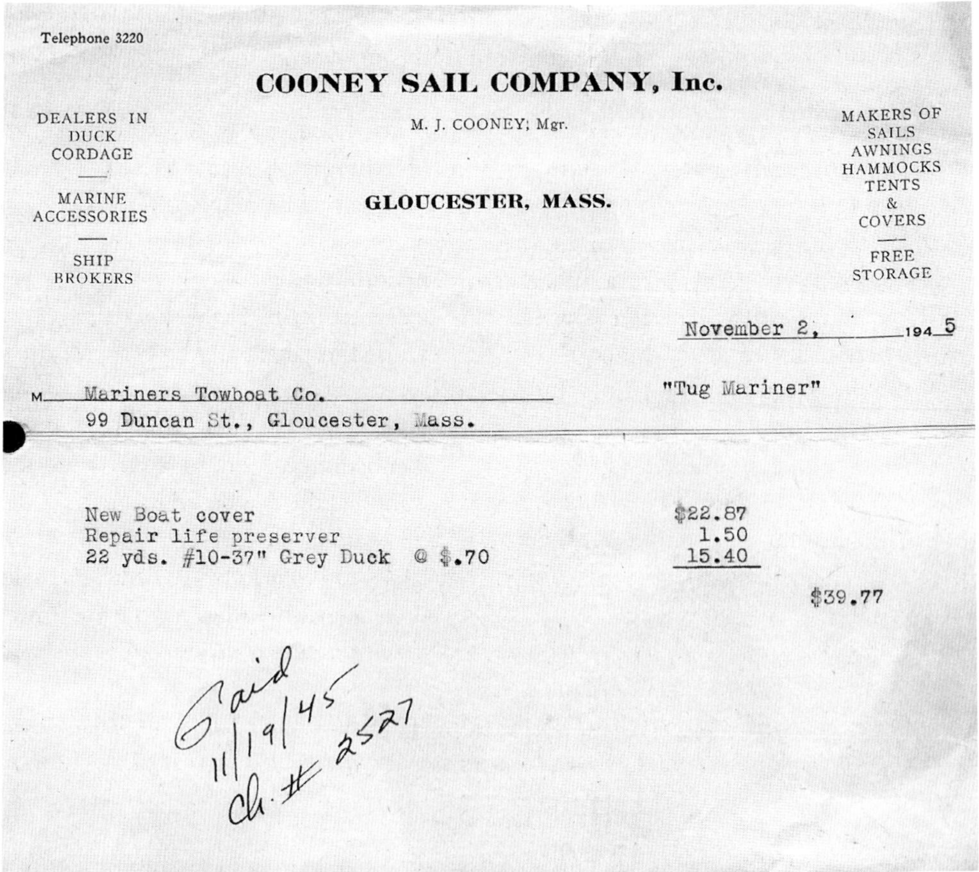

Telephone 3220

COONEY SAIL COMPANY, Inc.

DEALERS IN
DUCK
CORDAGE

MARINE
ACCESSORIES

SHIP
BROKERS

M. J. COONEY; Mgr.

GLOUCESTER, MASS.

MAKERS OF
SAILS
AWNINGS
HAMMOCKS
TENTS
&
COVERS

FREE
STORAGE

November 2,   194_5_

M___ Mariners Towboat Co.   "Tug Mariner"
    99 Duncan St., Gloucester, Mass.

New Boat cover $22.87
Repair life preserver   1.50
22 yds. #10-37" Grey Duck @ $.70   15.40

                                        $39.77

Paid
11/19/45
Ch. # 2527

A 1945 receipt from Cooney Sail Co., Inc., of Gloucester. *J.L. Sutherland.*

Depending on the seasons, sails were sewn by machine from great 40-yard bolts of either heavy- or light-weight canvas. The boltropes and thimbles on the sail edges were hand sewn with big triangular needles with a leather palm. Beeswax was sometimes used to lessen the pressure needed to sew.

There were other facilities worth mentioning in the care and upkeep of the fleet. Of course, as with all these vessels, some means had to be developed to haul them out for periodic maintenance of the hulls. There were three main facilities for this purpose, and dozens of men were employed at each one.

One was located at the extreme end of Rocky Neck, in East Gloucester, appropriately called Rocky Neck Marine Railways. It had two tracks, and provided all the necessary underwater services for the fleet. Scrubbing and painting of the hulls increased the speed of the vessels, which was necessary to get to market. Vessels took a beating in the winter and, at times, needed a great deal of caulking and refastening. The smell of pine tar from the caulking yarn permeated the yards just about every day. Choice of bottom paint for most of all floating crafts was the world-famous Tarr & Wonsons copper paint. Gloucester's Paint Factory is a beloved landmark and, although out of business, its outer features remain the same.

Two major railways were located at the end of then Duncan and Wharf Streets. One was Parkhurst, a two-track railway to the south of the gas company. Elias and Parker Burnham operated the other railway just north of the same gas company. Burnham's was built around 1849, and has been in business ever since.

When my dad worked there, a junk man made periodic visits. The alley leading down to the yard was paved with street stone, very slippery granite blocks, never to wear out. One day, this junk man, with his horse and team, tried to get up the slope to the street above, with no avail. He was whipping the horse something wicked, and the horse couldn't get traction.

Well, my dad had to put a stop to that, so he climbed the wagon, took the whip, and broke it into pieces. He then took the bitt in hand and led the team up the ramp with no trouble at all, admonishing the driver not to do that again in his presence.

These properties were purchased in October 2000, by the Gloucester Maritime Heritage Center. It operates a semi–hands-on exhibit of fish, lobsters, and other marine life. There is also a small but impressive museum, and as time and funds permit, the center and museum will grow to encompass all marine activities.

The marine railway supports boat repair and small boat building, and among the vessels currently berthed there is the 121-foot schooner *Adventure*, built in Essex, Massachusetts,

GLOUCESTER, MASS. April 1, 1946

Tug Boat Mariner & Owners

PARKHURST MARINE RAILWAY CO.
5 WHARF STREET

HAULING OUT - REPAIRING - PAINTING
FISHING VESSELS AND YACHTS

FOUR MARINE WAYS   TELEPHONE CONNECTION

Apr.	5	2½ lbs. 1/4 X 2 Plate Nails		50	

A 1946 receipt from Parkhurst Marine Railway Co. *J.L. Sutherland.*

Docking at Burnham's Railway in 1946. *J.L. Sutherland.*

in 1926, and the last of the great fleet of bank dory trawlers. This vessel was skippered by a salty individual, aptly nicknamed "In and out (Leo) Hynes," because he cleared the dock for another trip, almost as the last fish was sold. Also, there was the *Vincie N.*, the last wooden eastern rigged otter trawler out of this port. The *Vincie N.* was originally named the *Uncle Guy*, built in Rockland, Maine, in 1936. Her official measurements are: 86 feet in length, 18 feet breadth, 9 feet depth, and an engine of 180 horse power.

When both hauling cradles were operated by steam, my father was the last engineer to work there. Electric power is now used for hauling vessels, and one track has been discontinued. Time and again, I would go into the engine room and watch the big "Brown" steam engine go back and forth, with its 18-inch-by-8-foot flywheel and leather belt turning the gears that hauled the vessels. What a sight indeed!

As the saying goes, "the past is history." This adage aptly fits the part of Gloucester's marine history as it pertains to the great sailing fishing vessels, and it has been covered *ad infinitum.*

Some authors mentioned much about the evolution of travel that occurred in the early 1800s, about the stagecoaches from Boston, to Eastern Railroad's extension that ended in Rockport.

The improvement in the rail systems, roads, and Ford's Model T, with its internal combustion engine, was making its presence felt. It was a blow that the steamboat excursion and commercial business could not overcome.

The diesel engine, installed in the fishing vessels in the teens and early twenties, was instrumental in that fishing vessels could go directly to the newly erected fish pier, built at Boston around 1923, and sell their catches. The dependence on the steamboat to freight their fish to the "Hub" had finally come to an end; it is time to visit the steam-powered vessels that used the port of Gloucester.

GRUB AND WATER

Few would argue that food is as important an item as anything that comes aboard any Grand Bank vessel, except, perhaps, fishhooks and tub trawls. Food, to a fisherman, can only mean "grub." Now, where the word "grub" came from, is vague, something related to a grub hoe. The dictionary refers to the word as slang for "to provide with food." In fishermen terms, it takes that meaning to extremes. Changing the phrase a bit, to "dig in" is to start eating, usually with a vengeance. "Grub" is the universal term used for food on any vessel.

On all vessels, the captain is the sole ruler, but he had better not interfere with the cook's work. On Grand Bankers, the only men left aboard when the dory trawls are set are the captain, mate, and the cook. The cook was considered by many fishermen to be the most important man aboard, perhaps with the begrudging exception of the captain. The cook ordered the food, but the owner, with a critical eye on the future profits and looking over his shoulder, would give a slight nudge to the conservative side. With a somewhat veiled threat, he may volunteer a suggestion to ease up a bit. A good cook would have nothing to do with any urging. Fishermen knew food, and it had better be good and plentiful—ask any hand who had shipped out.

Aerial view of Boston Fish Pier. *Fairchild Surveys Inc.*

Steel otter trawler *Esther M* in Boston. *Fairchild Surveys Inc.*

To list the food needed for 26 or 28 men aboard an offshore dory-trawling vessel early in the 1900s would take too long to put on paper. Some salt banking trips were as long as two or more months. Provisions filled the forecastle lockers and were all but empty when arriving in port. (Grocers loved this.) A few items will give an idea of what it was like: say, two, maybe three barrels of flour, same with sugar; several five-pound pails of lard (this was for bread making), which was a staple no fisherman would do without. Then the other items include yeast, baking soda, salt, fresh pepper, vegetables for the first of the trip, canned goods, short barrels, kegs of corned beef still in the brine, slabs of bacon and pork, and fruits that would keep (like lemons and limes)—in fact everything wholesome and plenty of it. A type of soda cracker called "hardtack" was a needed staple; usually this item came locally from Hubbard's, a well-known Gloucester bakery. A full belly kept the men happy. Some would say that the amount of "grub" taken aboard put the vessel down by the head. Today, with only a few men to feed for a few days, the cook is not quite so important. Day boats might have pasta, a boiled dinner, or even fish.

The men had to have foul weather gear, and one supplier was D.O. Frost Co. There were others in the same business, and all made a living. Remember, there were 400 to 500 vessels, with 25 or 30 men to feed and clothe—they were the bread and butter of these supporting industries.

Offshore line trawler with dories and modern otter trawlers. *Fairchild Surveys Inc.*

The vessels also had to have decent potable water. The water tanks were usually locat-ed below the floors of the forecastle, and usually made of cypress. The tanks varied from 4,000 to over 5,000 gallons. There were multiple water boats to service their needs. *Eli Cleaves* was one of many. It was sail driven and looked similar to the "cat boats." They were nothing but a floating water tank, and if the cypress tanks were not cleaned, the water was terrible. Joe Garland's publication *Gloucester on the Wind* has a "landlubber" quoted as saying in 1879, "the water [*Eli*] supplied was absolutely disgusting." However, fishermen, in those days, could stomach most anything. The last two water boats that were around were the *Wanderer* and the *Wenham Lake*.

The latter, I remember well. John and Herbert Wennerberg, who, in 1902, lived on Mt. Pleasant Avenue in East Gloucester, operated it. Herbie lived with his father and their last address was on Plum Street in East Gloucester. Like all other water boats, it was originally a sail-driven sloop. In later days, it was propelled by a "one lunger" Lathrop gas engine. Herb started the engine with a flip of the flywheel, and with a controlling switch at the gangway, he made the direct connecting engine go in either direction by manipulating the switch.

I must tell about Herb's dog. It was a curly haired, nondescript mongrel, and had a bath only when he fell overboard, which was not often. Herb would take him aboard every day, high tide or low, down the wharf ladder. The dog would get handouts whenever they stopped at a vessel. At the end of the day, Herb would make his usual stop at Hyman Visnick's watering hole in East Gloucester square, and as his custom, have a snort or two. He would pour a beer into a pie plate on the floor for the dog. When time to leave, the half-stoned pup would lead the way across the square for home. Now that was a sight!

STEAMBOATS OF THE
NORTH SHORE

2

Gloucester authors, and writers in general, were more interested in the great fishing vessels rather than steamboats, and perhaps rightly so. These vessels captured the imagination of the public, and it seemed relatively easy to transcribe the historic and gripping hardships associated with the fishing industry. Commercial steamboating, on the other hand, was dull and repetitious. Their trips were an everyday occurrence and came and went on prescribed schedules. For the most part, nothing of great importance ever occurred to them, but they deserve their day in history.

Passenger and freight service for the North Shore first came into being around 1844. This new type of transportation to the North Shore was fast coming into its own and the first routes were short ones to Winthrop, Nahant, and Salem. Later ads in the local papers extolled the new and efficient mode of travel with a two-hour sail to Gloucester on the waters of the North Shore. For only 50¢ to a $1.00 round trip, this was a bargain. There were a few times when the return fare was reduced to 75¢ to attract a greater number of passengers. A layover of three hours gave passengers time to explore the fishing port and the budding art colony, plus, the salt air was free of the dust and dirt common on the shore rides.

There were many steamers that plied their trade on the North Shore. From around the year 1841 until the last regularly scheduled trip by the *Myrtle II* in 1931, at least 25 passenger and freight vessels came and went, some only once in a while.

The list of paddle-wheel steamers that serviced the North Shore between 1849 and 1870 is extensive. The first to service the Gloucester route was the three-year-old *Yacht*, operated by one Menemon Sanford on a haphazard service to Cape Ann around 1847. In 1869, the Boston & Gloucester Steamship Co. was incorporated and regular year-round service began. *Mystic*, built at New London, Connecticut, in 1852, inau-

Boston & Gloucester Steamship Co. freight shed at steamboat wharf in Gloucester in the 1900s. *J.L. Sutherland.*

gurated the service and ran until 1863. *Ulysses: S.W.* was built in Boston in 1863, for the Boston and Nahant Route. *Regulator* was so named, according to the publication *Evolution of Cape Ann Roads,* "because it intended, by low fares, to 'regulate' the rates charged by the railroads"; but the steamer only ran for one season—so much for the *Regulator. Charles Houghton, Nathaniel P. Banks, Emeline, Stamford,* and *Admiral* followed it.

Competition increased after the Civil War and Captain W.W. Colt, who had been steamboating on Long Island Sound, acquired the Boston & Gloucester Steamship Company in 1869. He entered the steamers *Escort* and *W.W. Colt* to run between Boston, Salem, and Gloucester. Three years later, he added the *Mischief, Fanny,* and *Three Brothers.* Some of these earlier vessels were taken by the government for service in the war, or went out of business because of competitors, and of course, the added cost of operating inefficient vessels.

Before ending the phase of side-wheel-propelled vessels on the North Shore, I believe it is important to inject here the horrific tale of the side-wheeler *Portland* as a case in point where a different means of construction and the propelling of steamships deserved serious consideration.

Boston & Gloucester Steamship Co.
WHARF, FOOT OF PEARCE STREET
GLOUCESTER, MASS.

Stationery of the Boston and Gloucester (B & G) Steamship Company. *J.L. Sutherland.*

THE *PORTLAND*

The steamship *Portland* was built in 1890 by the New England Shipbuilding Corporation in Bath, Maine, for the Portland Steamship Company. She was 281 feet long and had a 42-foot beam, with paddle boxes adding to the beam for a total of 59 feet. Her draft, less than 11 feet on a wooden hull, like many of the side-wheelers of her day, was comparatively shallow for her length and was best suited to work in sheltered inland waters and rivers. Many of the aforementioned side-wheel-propelled vessels ended up being successful in the relative safety of our inland waters.

Her run from India wharf in Boston to Portland and return, over a period of about eight years, was a relatively safe ocean trip. The vessel was inspected every year by the U.S. Steamboat Inspection Service and was given a clean bill of health every time.

The walking beam engine, a proven form of engine, had a critical drawback. It was heavy and massive, and the exposed rocker beam stood some 15 feet above her third deck, giving the hull a high center of gravity. There are not many people alive that know the workings of a walking beam engine, or even what one looks like. In as short a description as possible, this is the action. In reality, it is no different than an ordinary marine steam engine in that it takes steam from a boiler, and in a double acting engine, admits it at the right time into either the top or bottom of a cylinder, to get what is called a "double acting," with two power strokes to a revolution. Through an eccentric, steam is admitted to either end of a cylinder. Then a series of links opens a valve to the top or bottom of the cylinder at the proper time. The action produced is similar to the pumps on oil wells, except that the beam has the crank fulcrum that turns the paddle wheels. The photo of a typical beam ending is in essence, the same in all side-wheelers, including the *Portland*.

All side-wheelers with this type of engine were susceptible to serious rolling of the hull, and the North Atlantic was, and is, even when on its best behavior, not the calmest of waters. The winter, with its storms and endless ground swells, had the side-wheels on one side deep into the sea; conversely, the other side was hardly immersed.

The storm that overtook the *Portland* was known in advance. A weather advisory had been issued before she sailed, indicating "east to northeast gales with heavy snow tonight. Wind west to northwest tomorrow and colder." Now, the North Atlantic is no place to be with gale-force winds expected. Captain Hollis H. Blanchard considered the forecast, but thought he could make the nine-hour trip safely. And so it was, on that evening of Sunday, November 27, 1898, history was made.

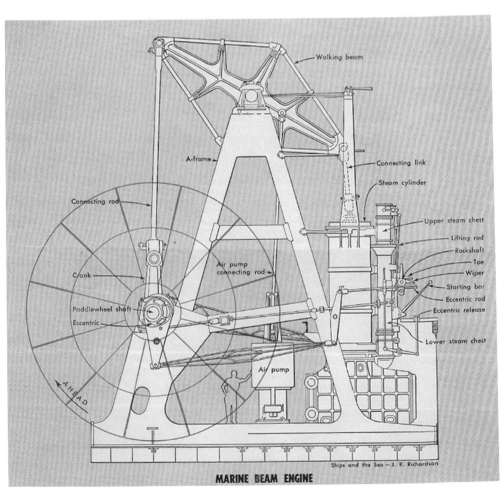

MARINE BEAM ENGINE

Diagram of the marine walking beam engine. Ships and the Sea *by J.R. Richardson.*

At 7:00 p.m., Captain Blanchard made a fateful decision and headed out to sea. No one in Portland knew if the vessel had left Boston or if it did, if it sought shelter in a harbor along the way. The officials of the Portland Steam Packet Co. insisted that they phoned the Boston office and urged that the vessel remain in port. Interviews with other interests said that the company ordered him to sail.

There was little wind; the sea was deceptively calm. At 8:30 p.m., the vessel was off Thatcher's Island, about 25 miles out of Boston. Within an hour or slightly more, the weather front with snow falling was upon the ship. Some fishing vessels heading for safety in Gloucester saw what they believed to be a steamer laboring in mounting seas.

What happened after that is pure conjecture. After the steamer rounded Cape Ann, and the relative lee of its shore, the full effect of the gales that were soon to come across the broad reach of Ipswich Bay soon whipped up an angry sea.

The last vessel to sight the steamer was the *Ruth M. Martin*, laboring herself to get to Provincetown. A surf man entered into the log of the Race Point Lifesaving Station this message: "At 5:45 a.m. I heard Stmr. blow four whistle distress signals. Called my crew and looked for steamer but could find nothing."

In retrospect, any number of scenarios surfaced as to the destruction of this vessel. It is not unlikely that some form of driftwood got caught up in a paddle wheel and in so doing crippled the engine and left the vessel broadside to the terrible sea. There was the possibility of the paddle boxes breaking up in the rough seas. The fact that the hull was constructed of wood means that stress may have opened the hull to the elements. Any of these situations would spell doom in short order. Given the horrendous situation of the storm, lifeboats, even if successfully launched, would have provided only a few minutes of safety.

By Sunday evening, debris from the ship, including a cork-filled life jacket with the words "Str. *Portland*," had washed ashore on the northern tip of Cape Cod. There were battered pieces of wreckage, and the bodies (21 in the first few days) totaled 40 within weeks. The exact number of passengers, estimated at around 176 plus the crew, was not officially determined; a passenger list was not mandatory in those days. The number of last-minute boarders, and those worried about the storm that decided to stay in Boston rather than chance the trip, are always vague.

For years, the wreckage of the *Portland* was never located, raising further questions about where the ship went down. It was not until 1989 that two researchers, using side-scan sonar, revealed that they had found an object in waters 300 to 400 feet deep some 20 miles north of Cape Cod. While that area seems likely as the *Portland's* resting place, up until now, no definitive proof has been offered by items recovered or photographed. Although the exact location is a well-kept secret, photos of a vessel have been taken and they clearly show a rocking beam engine, boilers, and double smokestacks. The hull, what there is of it, is resting upright on a sandy bottom. Until the wreck is researched, it is an excellent candidate for the vessel *Portland*. A plaque dedicated to the passengers, crew, and the ship in the town of Truro on Cape Cod lists the ship as going down about seven miles east of Cape Race light, but, at the time, that was just a guess. The hurricane blizzard of 1898 left the Northeast paralyzed for days, but it will always be remembered as the *Portland* gale of 1898.

As recent as early 2004 a letter was discovered concerning the *Portland* disaster. The letter was written December 3, 1898, by C.F. Williams, the company agent of the Portland Steamship Co., to John F. Liscomb, the company's general manager in Portland. The letter referred to Williams telling George Barton, the watchman, that he had told Captain Blanchard to wait for the 9 o'clock weather report. Seven p.m. was the departure time, and Blanchard was bound to go on time and did not want to wait. It was observed that Williams, the company agent, was only telling his side of the events. It could be construed that he was covering up his own tracks.

In a dramatic fashion, this event hastened the demise of the paddle-wheel steamers on the Atlantic and the introduction of the screw propeller. In all fairness, while this particular incident did not in itself cause the end of this type of propulsion on the open waters of oceans, it gave thought that the design of future vessels should be constructed of iron or steel. All of these early steamers were side-wheelers, and relatively of shallow six- to nine-foot draft. "Snags" and driftwood were the bane of the paddle wheels, causing much anxiety to the captains and engineers, as the operators of steamboats on the inland rivers could attest to. The deeper draft of the newer ships gave better stability, and propeller propulsion was safe from most driftwood.

Propeller propulsion would come into general use around 1863. There would be several vessels to sport this "newest means of propulsion." Those that followed were *George A. Chaffee* (1870), *City of Gloucester* (1883), *Mascotte* (1885), *Cape Ann* (1885), *City of Haverhill* (1902), *Myrtle II* (1901), and finally the *Monhegan* (1903). The *Governor Prence* (1917) and the *Roseway* (1918) were motor vessels.

A few of the earlier vessels plied their respective routes and then faded from the records. Perhaps their fate lies somewhere in the many journals produced over the years. In the early days of newspaper items, if a steamer did not blow up, burn, or wreck on some reef or lee shore, it was hardly worth a line. A list of twelve or more steamers was recorded by various publications between 1844 and 1863. Sometime later, for one reason or another, the North Shore route was, for all intents and purposes, abandoned to the Boston & Gloucester Steamship Co. as the only adequate supplier of freight and passenger service.

The Boston & Gloucester Steamship Co. purchased the *George A. Chaffee*, which was built in Connecticut in 1870. For the next 19 years, she made her runs from Boston to Gloucester until 1895. After 25 years, it was time to look around for another vessel. Captain Nehemiah Proctor (11 Chestnut Street, Gloucester), Captain E.S. Young, and for a time, Captain Henry Godfrey (of Lubec, Maine) were also in command of the *Chaffee* while the vessel was in the service of the Boston & Gloucester Steamship Co. Incorporated in 1869, the long-lived Boston & Gloucester Steamship Co. lasted until 1926, when the company finally sold its interests to the Massachusetts Bay Steamship Co.

It is important in the interest of history that some greater time be spent with the two later steamers that serviced the North Shore and particularly Gloucester. With the expansion of the excursion business, new and better-equipped vessels for year-round service had to be considered. The Boston & Gloucester Steamship Co. secured the services of the J.D. Leary Co. of Brooklyn, New York, to build a freight and passenger vessel for the North Shore. This vessel was to be christened the *City of Gloucester*, and her measurements were to be a weight of 561 tons, 142.5 feet in length, 28-foot beam, and 11.6-foot depth; her official number was 126139.

THE *CITY OF GLOUCESTER*

The year was 1883, and she made her maiden trip from Gloucester to Boston on July 27, under the command of Captain E.S. Young, formally the master of the *George A. Chaffee*. For the next 43 years, she gave remarkable service.

In the later years, when my father was acting second engineer on the *City*, he reviewed the particulars of this vessel's history. Oddly enough, instead of being steel or iron, the *City*'s hull was constructed of the best grade of New England white oak. Construction was to be substantial to stand the rigors of a winter sailing. Her propulsion equipment was a compound engine, and a single fire tube boiler, both furnished and installed by Pusey & Jones of Wilmington, Delaware.

S.S. *City of Gloucester* under way in Gloucester Harbor. *Steamship Historical Society of America Collection # 7255 R.L. Graham.*

Starboard view of S.S. *City of Gloucester* at Boston's Central Wharf, 1883. *Steamship Historical Society of America Collection # 4237.*

S.S. *City of Gloucester* hauled out in Boston, 1883. *Steamship Historical Society of America Collection #2878 R.L. Graham.*

It is reasonably safe to say, having looked at photos of her, that one would not be alone in describing her as one of the ugliest vessels afloat: high sided, little or no sheer, plumb stem, a modified cruiser stern, low squat deck and wheelhouse, and a funnel much to high. As viewed on the Atlantic Works Railways in East Boston, she looked like a huge block of wood.

I have to say, the designer, Lord rest his soul, surely must have been in his cups when he applied his pen to paper. Still, one has to give the designer some measure of credit; she was built to last. Her winter runs in 1902 had her breaking ice in the harbor.

In the publication *Evolution of the Cape Ann Roads* and other periodicals, the *City* led to a good deal of talk around town that she had never failed in her appointed runs, but there are a couple of incidents in her career that are worth mentioning. On her maiden voyage to Boston on July 27, 1883, with the Gloucester Cornet Band for entertainment and Jonny Morgan as caterer, the sea was so rough that she had to turn back at Half Way Rock.

On June 26, 1924, while taking the Ancient & Honorable Artillery Company on an excursion 12 miles seaward, she was visited by a sudden summer thunderstorm, and a bolt of lightning shattered her main mast. It was during the age of Prohibition, so I suppose some could view it as some sort of omen.

This workhorse was primarily used as a freighter, although at times it would fill in with excursions on weekends in the summer. The soon-to-come *Cape Ann* would only carry a

S.S. *City of Gloucester* breaking ice in Gloucester, 1902. *Steamship Historical Society of America Collection # 2876 R.L. Graham.*

Another view of S.S. *City of Gloucester* at Boston's Central Wharf, 1883. *Steamship Historical Society of America Collection # 4807 R.L. Graham.*

S.S. *City of Gloucester* at Boston's Central Wharf, 1883. *Steamship Historical Society of America Collection # 4239 R.L. Graham.*

moderate amount of freight up forward, but the *City* was built to transport all manner of goods to and from Boston. This "greyhound" of the North Shore, with a cruising speed of between 12 and 13 knots, carried its cargo winter and summer. The steaming time from Boston to Gloucester was something to be relied upon despite all manner of weather. On the run to Boston, she carried a full fare of fresh fish plus other fish-related products, such as cod liver oil, dried and boxed cod, and other mixed fish products. This was the daily fare for years. The return trip to Gloucester included dry goods, groceries, even some odd furniture, and, of course, a few passengers.

Toward the end of her career, the *City*'s schedule was more or less haphazard. The directors reluctantly realized that the trains and trucks were taking their toll. It was also a fact that most of the newer fishing vessels, relying on their own diesel power, could go to Boston and deliver their fish directly to the producers at the new fish pier. The end to the existence of the *City* was now only a few years away.

In the early eighteenth century, travel from town to town was by stagecoach and mostly by way of winding, rough, and dusty roads. Travel time from Boston to Gloucester, some 30 miles away, took the best part of the daylight hours. There were two trips scheduled each day, and inns were placed at strategic spots for food and rest. At eight miles an hour, sometimes less, it was not a nice smooth ride. Most, if not all of the passengers, had business to attend to, and as the trip progressed, so did their discontent of this mode of transportation. As for the traveler seeking a few days of rest and relaxation at the North Shore's hotels and beaches, it was roundly criticized as bone jarring and dirty. There had to be a better way of travel, but it was slow in coming.

It was around 1838 when Eastern Railroad initiated its first of many expansions into the areas covered by the stagecoaches. Passenger travel time was greatly improved, most schedules were kept within reason and, to a degree, smoother rides exacted some measure of pleasure.

The one glaring drawback was the smoke and cinders from the steam engines, which reached into every car. On arriving at their final destination, passengers opted for a quick bath and a complete change of clothes. It was not uncommon to hear the crunch of cinders under foot in the aisles of the passenger cars. Far into the twentieth century, this discomfort continued to plague the rail commuters.

Railroad freight, on the other hand, was now competitive, and provided a quick and efficient delivery of goods; shipping could be had at a more reasonable rate. It was not uncommon to see large consignments of fish and fish-related products put in the freight cars at the Gloucester station that accompanied the passenger cars. In most cases, there were up to 16 trains a day, and delivery to Boston took less than an hour.

Another critical development that hastened the end of most excursion vessels was the automobile. More and more of the faithful passengers soon realized that one could tour the countryside at their leisure. Times of departure and arrivals were a thing of the past; travelers could come and go as they pleased. Operating costs of these steamers were eating away at the meager profits.

S.S. *City of Gloucester* at Boston's Central Wharf, *c.* 1900. *Steamship Historical Society of America Collection #3627-B Acores.*

The end came for the *City*, and without so much of a whimper. The records show that the *City* made her last and final voyage for the Boston & Gloucester Steamship Co. on July 18, 1925. The master of the *City of Gloucester* on her last sailing from Gloucester to Boston was Captain Fred H. Pray, the mate was Loren A. Jacobs, and the engineer was Charles W. Bumpus.

Moored for over a year in Boston near the Congress Street Bridge, the *City* was purchased on December 7, 1927, by the Thames River Line, Inc., based in Connecticut. The company renamed the vessel the *Thames* and operated her in freight service between New York, Bridgeport, and New London until 1930, when she was reported as destroyed by fire on Long Island Sound. There is no record if there was loss of life or serious injury in the event. It is better to have been sent to a watery grave than to lie rotting at some nondescript pier in the end; so much for the *City of Gloucester*.

THE *CAPE ANN*

But let us now return to a time some 12 years after the *City* was built. Another vessel was ordered by the Boston & Gloucester Steamship Co. In the late 1800s, the excursion business was in its heyday. A meeting was held, and someone in the company must surely have mused: "In all due respect, let us have a vessel that looks the part!"

S.S. *Cape Ann* arriving in Gloucester Harbor *c.* 1905. *Steamship Historical Society of America Collection # 2742-B.*

S.S. *Cape Ann* underway in Gloucester, 1895. *Steamship Historical Society of America Collection # 4915.*

The directors awarded a contract in 1884 to the Neafie and Levy Ship and Engine Building Co. of Philadelphia to replace the then-aging *George W. Chaffee.* The new vessel was to be built of steel, and the design of the vessel was left to Benjamin Post, superintendent engineer of the Metropolitan Steamship Co. of Boston.

The *Cape Ann* was built in less than five months at an estimated cost of $100,000, and was ready on time. From the moment she took to her salty element until the day she finally left the port of Gloucester in 1917 on a towline for New York, she was observed as a thing of beauty and was admired by all who witnessed her countless comings and goings. Without a doubt, this vessel was to be the pride of Gloucester; it deserves some detailed attention.

She was launched on April 6, 1895, and christened *Cape Ann* by Miss Agnes Merchant, the daughter of Edgar Merchant, the company agent. The *Cape Ann's* measurements were 185 x 28 x 13.5 feet. Her official number was 127074. She was 719 gross tons, 598 net tons, and had screw propulsion. The officers on the *Cape Ann* at the launching and subsequent trip to Boston were Captain Henry M. Godfrey (of Lubec, Maine), Pilot George Bearse (Boston), First Mate Leo Campbell (Boston), Chief Engineer Frank Fowles (Gloucester), Assistant Engineer Frank Daniels (Somerville, Massachusetts), and Steward Herbert Lane (Everett, Massachusetts). The late Gordon Thomas, marine historian of some note, in his excellent review, gave some of her particulars and appointments in a June 1952 *Gloucester Daily Times* article that are worth repeating. According to Thomas,

> The ship left the yards, in the afternoon of June 5, 1895, and arrived at Central Wharf in Boston, at 1:25 p.m., on the 7th of June. On June 10th, the 25th anniversary of the company's corporation, she made her gala appearance in Gloucester . . . Everyone who was anyone was aboard, and it was said that at her arrival, (of course well advertised in advance), she was greeted with the sound of every whistle in the harbor. This trip, and the many after, took exactly two hours, and after securing to the pier at the foot of Duncan Street, the public was invited aboard.

Added information came from my father who was an oiler and acting second engineer on the *Cape Ann* at the time from 1910 to 1917 (working under Chief Eugene Connolly's license), and may be of some value to the local historical buffs.

The *Cape Ann* was used mostly as a summer excursion and freight vessel, and was laid up at the steamboat wharf then located at the foot of Duncan Street in the winter months.

There were times when she would be used on special outings. On June 17, 1895, with nearly twice the registered capacity aboard (she was registered for 1,000), the paying public enjoyed a sail around Massachusetts Bay and about the shores of Cape Ann. The throng greatly exceeded her lifeboat capacity, inviting disaster. The marine inspectors were, to say the least, somewhat derelict in their appointed duties. As an added feature the Gloucester City Band furnished entertainment. The prices of the tickets were 50¢ for adults, 25¢ for children; for a two- to three-hour sail, this was considered a bargain. It must be said that in the early 1900s, 50¢ was considered a tidy sum.

S.S. *Cape Ann*, outward-bound from Gloucester, 1895. *Steamship Historical Society of America Collection #2742-C.*

A 1,500-horsepower vertical compound-condensing engine, built by the same company, powered the *Cape Ann.* At the time, an oceangoing towboat was being constructed in the same yard alongside of the *Cape Ann.* When the tug was ready for an engine, the only one available was the one designated for the *Cape Ann.* A deal was made, and the tug got it. When it was time for installing an engine in the *Cape Ann,* the only one available was a larger, 1,500-horsepower machine, at no extra cost. It was about 300 horsepower more than the design called for and somewhat larger in frame, but with some small adjustment to the engine bed and a larger steam condenser, it fitted in nicely.

As it turned out, the engine gave the vessel, with a clean bottom, a speed of 16 knots without pushing, and over the years, running in and out of Boston Harbor, it was noted at the time that not one of the so-called "Nantasket Greyhounds" could match her speed from Central Wharf in Boston to the "Deer Island Bug light." You will learn more of these impromptu "races" as you read along.

Giving due respect to the notations in Dana A. Story's excellent publication *The Shipbuilders of Essex,* it was noted that on July 4, 1900, the 165-foot passenger steamer *Cape Cod* (built in Essex) was on her trials in and about Boston Harbor and then headed to Gloucester. On the way back to Boston, the *Cape Cod* had an "informal" race with the *Cape Ann* and was first to arrive at the dock, reaching a speed of 14.7 knots.

Without going into a great deal of detail, from what my father related to me about the speed of the *Cape Ann,* the cruising speed was in the vicinity of 15 knots, the shaft

S.S. *Cape Ann* arriving in Gloucester Harbor in 1895. *Steamship Historical Society of America Collection # 4961 R.L. Graham.*

turning 145 to 150 turns. When any "race" was in progress, and there were many, 16 knots or better was reached, the shaft turning at 160 to 165 turns.

Referring back to the late historian, Gordon Thomas, in his excellent article in the *Gloucester Daily Times* of June 14, 1952, he stated the knots *Cape Ann* was able to achieve as 16. One must assume that he meant cruising speed. Under the circumstances, it would be hard for one to concede that the *Cape Cod* was the faster vessel, when in her trials she made only 14.7 knots, and given the designer's promise of only 15 knots.

My father said that when the boiler was fired up to its limit, and the main engine and the auxiliaries were working hard, it was all two firemen could do to keep up an acceptable head of steam. Indeed, in one year a record 47 firemen were employed, a lesser number in most of the later years. Some firemen lasted one trip and quit. Even with the ventilators on the upper boat deck forcing somewhat cooler Atlantic air down the airshafts, it was miserably hot in the furnace room.

Sometimes, when an impromptu race was in the offing, Captain Godfrey would pass the word to the engineer Connolly. The airtight doors and ventilators were secured and a forced draft of one to two pounds of pressure was built up. With the firing doors closed and the ash pit doors cracked open a bit, the added forced draft literally lifted the coals off the grates, and that really used up the fuel. For the deck crew and the passengers, this was great fun; for the firemen, well that was something else. The directors were unhappy when the coal bill was due to be paid, and eventually forcing of the boiler was frowned upon.

The 67-foot "saloon" on the main deck had the very best in appointments. There were numerous leather chairs of every description for the comfort of the passengers. Purple or blue velvet curtains adorned the many windows and ports of the saloon. Steam radiators were placed inconspicuously, so that comfort could be had in the coolest of weather. At one time there was even a small lunch counter where sandwiches, coffee, and other beverages could be purchased. Most of the passengers brought their own lunches or opted to eat at one of the many fine restaurants in the Gloucester area.

As can be seen in many of the early photos of this handsome vessel, the two tall masts served two purposes: they gave stability by slowing the roll of the vessel, and early photos of the *Cape Ann* showed that the masts were initially fitted with sails, including a jib. This practice was later discontinued due in a great part to the dependability of the propulsion system.

In a photo showing the *Cape Ann* when first arriving in Gloucester, the hull was painted all black, with a black funnel. This color scheme lasted for a short time. The lower hull was painted black with a gray band above the guardrail from the stern to the end of the saloon deck. Topsides were white. In 1901 or so, this color scheme was later changed to all white with some black, like the guardrails and masts. The funnel was buff. This turned out to be the color scheme when, in 1917, she eventually left Gloucester.

S.S. *Cape Ann* leaving Gloucester Harbor in 1895. *Steamship Historical Society of America Collection # 4913.*

Whatever the color, there was no mistaking the graceful lines when presented broad-side. She was a thing of beauty, whether underway or moored to the dock.

There you have as brief a history as possible of commercial steam vessels on the North Shore from about 1841 to 1931.

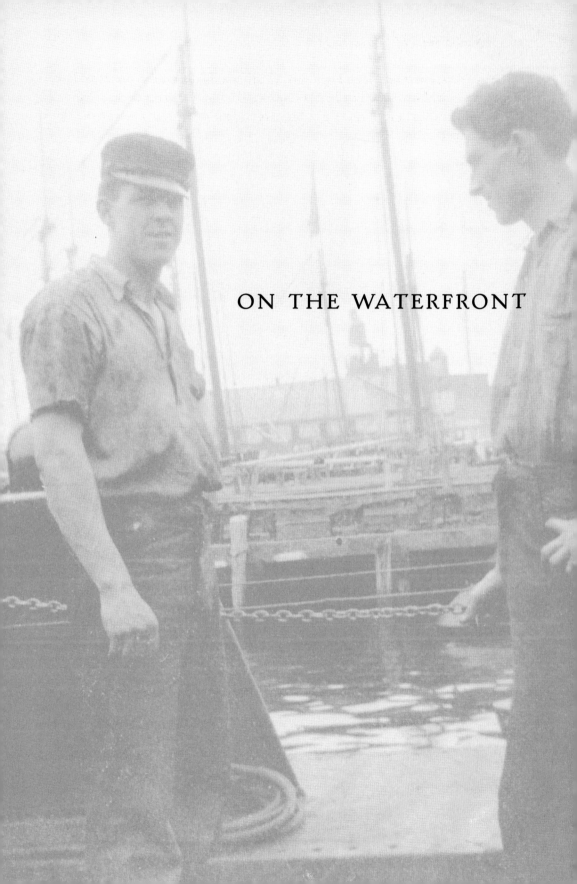

ON THE WATERFRONT

3

Ah, but not all of the labor in the early days was serious. There are a couple of rather humorous stories my father related to me about when he first came to "the States" from Scotland. The exact date of his arrival in this country is not known to me, but it has to be around 1907 or 1908, well before his employment on the *Cape Ann*.

Single at the time, my father went to work on the waterfront in Boston as a long-shoreman. This work at least gave him a bed and board, and it was steady. When un-loading the various ships that arrived from all over the world, there were times when some of the work gang needed, say, shoes. When a crate or box of shoes was swung over the dock, somehow the sling would slip, and down would come the load and split wide open. Well, the dock boss didn't want to hold up the progress, so he would order the men to clear away the material. In no time at all, most, if not all of the shoes would disappear. It was the same with clothing, rubber boots, or whatever happened to be needed, and most of the time the men could make out quite well.

Another time in the routine labor of their work, a situation would arise that would tickle the heart of many a Scotsman. Kegs of rum, brandy, or Scotch whisky, depend-ing where the ship hailed from, would be unloaded and put in a place of greater secu-rity, or so the agents of the consignment thought.

Wharves in those days were constructed on wooden pilings and planked in the usual way. Every so often, there would be a two-inch drain hole, and if a spill of some liquid occurred, or the wharf gang hosed down the pier, it would drain into the harbor waters below.

Now the sight of barrels of good rum, or better still, Scotch whisky, set the mind to wonderful thoughts. As the barrels were being deposited in their assigned places, someone would hang a length of rope or strip of cloth down the hole. This would

Sherman Ruth's Wharf was a typical wooden wharf, *c*.1940. *J.L. Sutherland.*

mark where this particular hole was from under the pier. Next, whatever barrel was selected was placed over that hole. This kind of merchandise would not be left around for longer than a day or night; one had to play out his hand early.

A dory or punt was secured, and a barrel, with a large open end, somewhat the equal to the volume of the "mother" barrel, was put aboard. The tide being at low ebb, the culprits headed under the wharf to seek out the telltale marker. Then quietly, an auger was inched up into the drain hole. A hole was bored into the keg or barrel above, and the deed was done.

My father said it was quite messy, but he thought the rewards were well worth it. After having emptied the barrel above, and with some critical sampling, they retired to some quiet place and bottled the stuff. With this kind of "merchandise" on their hands, one had many friends.

This is but a small sample in the life of a typical waterfront worker at the turn of the century. I have only touched on a minute portion of the daily activities. It wasn't all fun and games; the hours were long, the wages poor—he mentioned something like seven or eight dollars a day, but, like I said earlier, it was work and it put bread on the table. However, he decided that something more permanent with a chance to move up the ladder, as it were, toward a profession was the way to go.

It was in the years between 1910 and 1924 that my father became involved in the operation of the *Cape Ann* and the *City of Gloucester*. It was early in the year 1910 that he

William J. Sutherland (on the right) and a seaman on Steamboat Wharf in Gloucester, c. 1914. *J.L. Sutherland.*

made contact with personnel of the Boston & Gloucester Steamship Co. at 244 Atlantic Avenue. Later, after an interview my father was employed on the *Cape Ann* as an oiler. This covered a period of about seven years until the *Cape Ann* was sold in 1917. He then transferred to the *City of Gloucester* as an oiler and acting assistant engineer until 1920.

In those days, if you were at all competent and mechanically inclined, you could land a job in the engine room of one of the many vessels working the coast. For the time being, lacking a marine license was of small consequence; you could work off of the chief's license, if he was so inclined to let you.

His position in the engine room of the *City of Gloucester* afforded my father the golden opportunity to apply for his steamship-engineering license. He had a "hunch" that local freight steamers were on their way out for several reasons: the trains were running on a tighter schedule and at a more competitive rate and the rising costs of boat operations were cutting deep into the profits.

Now married, with four youngsters, my father thought it was time to get a position as engineer close to home. With all the steam towboats scurrying around Gloucester Harbor, it was natural to step into one of the positions as engineer. But first there was need for an engineer's certificate. As oiler and assistant engineer on the *Cape Ann* for seven years, and acquiring the experience to operate the plant under Chief Connolly's license, plus over six years on the *City of Gloucester* working under Chief Engineer Bumpus's license, this was all he needed to get his own certificate.

My father received several recommendations of his service to the company. One was from Chief Engineer Eugene Connolly on the steamer *Cape Ann* dated September 23, 1920. Another was from Chief Engineer Charles W. Bumpus. I also have a letter from Captain Larsen, master of the *City of Gloucester*, who recommended him highly as a "very good engineer" to anyone desiring the services of a conscientious, honest, reliable man.

He was ready for the test and qualified with a 92 percent—only one person with a higher average than him was listed. So on November 4, 1920, in the Boston office of the secretary of the First U.S. Civil Service District, located in the customhouse, my father was issued a marine steam engineer's license. The reserves or limitations on the document were as follows: "Chief Engineer, 2,500 H.P.; First Assistant, 5,000 H.P., Unlimited Second." By any standard, at a first sitting for the test, this was quite an achievement.

For a few years he continued on as assistant engineer on the *City of Gloucester* until January 31, 1924, when he joined up with Mariners' Towboat Co.

When both steamers were running before 1917, my dad worked freight as often as possible. Most times the *Cape Ann* docked somewhat earlier than the *City* on the south side of the steamboat wharf. After his duties were finished on the *Cape Ann*, he walked across to the east side of the pier and helped unload the *City*. The added income of another paycheck always came in handy.

When the *Cape Ann* was tied up for most of the winter months, steam still had to be kept up so nothing would freeze. As one of the watchmen on the *Cape Ann*, my father had the run of the ship. Captain Godfrey would use cigar boxes to keep all the used passenger tickets from the past season in his quarters. Father would go through box after box, and in the run of thousands of canceled tickets, he would get at least 40 good ones. These "Annie Oaklies" were good for a number of things, from a mess of fresh fish to a few snorts up at a local tavern, preferably at Howard Blackburn's emporium at 291–293 Main Street.

Gordon W. Thomas pointed out in his June 14, 1952 article that there were other incidents that he was familiar with in the years that *Cape Ann* steamed from port to port. One of the more significant events happened in the year 1899 (before my father's employment), when moored at her berth at Central Wharf in Boston. A fire broke out in the freight sheds of the company. Captain Godfrey, who had just turned in, smelled smoke. Fire was close aboard, and there was only a narrow walkway between the sheds and the ship. With no time to waste, he sounded the whistle, 12 short blasts or more, to call the fire department. The crew then proceeded to warp the vessel down to the end of the pier and out of harm's way. The fire was extinguished, and the incident was soon forgotten.

Another event mentioned in Thomas's article occurred on July 10, 1903. The *Cape Ann* was forced to anchor near the "Bug light" near Deer Island of Boston Harbor. Suddenly out of the fog came the fishing vessel *Alcina*, which struck the side of the

Notice of the average percentage
result for the Marine Engineer's
License test taken by William J.
Sutherland taken in 1920.
J.L. Sutherland.

S.S. *Cape Ann* underway in Gloucester, 1895. *Steamship Historical Society of America
Collection # 4914.*

Cape Ann. The steamer was unharmed, but *Alcina* suffered from a few broken planks and a few rail stanchions. (According to Story's *The Shipbuilders of Essex*, the 83-foot schooner *Alcina* was built in Essex in the spring of 1889 by James and Tarr.)

My father told me that when he first went to work in the engine room of the *Cape Ann*, he noticed the fractured engine cylinder support column, and asked the chief what happened to cause that kind of damage. The "incident" happened some years before when racing "full tilt" with a Nantasket-bound excursion steamer (the chief thought it was either the *Nantasket* or the *Plymouth*), when the *Cape Ann* "threw a blade." When one blade of a four-blade propeller was missing, the prop was out of balance. Chief Connolly told him "all hell broke loose." When on one of these speed runs, the chief was always at the throttle and cut the steam to the engine, but not before the violent shaking cracked one of the cast-iron cylinder support columns. He said at the time that he thought the engine would shake right off of its bed. Of course, with normal working pressure of between 200 and 225 pounds, with a sudden shut down of the engine, the safeties were blowing off in good style. (The boiler had duel safety valves.) The firemen raked out the embers from the fire spaces and hosed down everything in sight, but still the residual heat was making some steam, but at a reduced rate.

With all the shaking, it's a wonder the main ten-inch steam pipe from boiler to engine didn't rupture. If it had, surely all in the engine room and possibly the boiler room would have been killed or at the very least, severely scalded. I remember my dad telling me that the chief said "that it was the closest he'd been to going to hell."

Under dead slow speed, the *Cape Ann* returned to Central Wharf and discharged the disgruntled passengers. Then, they headed over to the Atlantic Works in East Boston to get hauled out. A new cast-iron propeller was installed and that was that. The cracked engine column was another thing. Steamboat inspectors were informed of the fracture, and with their approval, three pieces of railroad track, some six feet long, were fashioned, forming a sort of splint to the column and bound with wire. This repair was still in place when the *Cape Ann* was sold to the French interests in 1917.

There was yet another interesting event in the life of the *Cape Ann*. In the usual run from Boston to Gloucester and the return, time was of the essence. In those days, and in truth the same can be said to some extent today "towboat" landings were considered, in today's vernacular as "cool."

This time, coming into Central Wharf, the usual docking was contemplated with little or no fuss. The usual docking speed entering the slip was about a knot or a little more. Fast enough, but nothing to get excited about. It was usual to keep some "way" on the vessel for steerage reasons. What a surprise when Captain Godfrey gave the signal to reverse to Chief Connolly. He dutifully reversed the engine, but the *Cape Ann* kept right on her merry way.

Atlantic Avenue has changed considerably since the time being described. The avenue was built on filled portions of Boston Harbor waters. The supporting wall of

S.S. *Cape Ann* in Gloucester, 1895. *Steamship Historical Society of America Collection # 2742.*

the avenue was of granite blocks, probably quarried locally. Mostly to be used as a sidewalk on the waterside of the street, about 15 or 20 feet of good, stout, wooden pier work was created.

Coming in at a pretty good clip, as the good captain was wont to do, and had in fact done many times in the past, this was just another in a long line of uneventful dockings. Needless to say, the ship came to an abrupt halt, its nose cleaving the pier like Swiss cheese, and fetched up securely against the avenue. Fortunately, other than a few embarrassing moments, and a little paint peeled off of the bow plates, no real damage had been done, at least to the *Cape Ann*. Passengers and crew alike were thrown off of their feet; fortunately, no one was severely hurt. It was not unusual to see pedestrians leaning on the railing watching the steamer dock. Thankfully, this time no one was there. I would venture to say that the city repaired the woodwork and billed the company. What had happened was that the keeper bolt somehow came out, and the nut securing the screw to the shaft had worked itself off. With nothing to secure the screw in place, and with the resulting reversal of the rotation of the propeller, it simply slipped off the shaft.

After the passengers recovered from their fright and were put ashore, the tugs of the Boston Towboat Co. arrived and towed the *Cape Ann* over to the Atlantic Works at East Boston to be hauled out and a spare wheel fitted. Floating dry docks were not used at this yard, so it was a slow trip up the ways. Imagine the surprise when, as the hull dried out, here was the four-bladed cast-iron propeller hanging on the bitter end of the shaft and lodged against the rudderpost. It took no time at all to make a new key and nut, reset the screw on the shaft, and be on their way.

THE END OF THE
COMPANY

4

As in all enterprises, there is a beginning and an end. For 22 years, the *Cape Ann* plied its designated course day in and day out. If the number of passengers that enjoyed the trip on this handsome vessel were totaled up, it would be safe to wager that many thousands upon thousands of satisfied customers had availed themselves of a day well spent. At the prevailing price of $1 for a round-trip ticket and 50¢ for a one-way ticket, it gave the average person a little time away from the bustle of city life. But times change, as they must. Day-trippers were acquiring automobiles and had other things to do, and the directors soon realized the handwriting on the wall.

The company was approached by J.W. Elwell & Co. of New York, agents for the French government. They purchased the *Cape Ann* for the tidy sum of $200,000. This offer was not to be sneezed at, for it was twice the cost of the 22-year-old vessel when it was built. Documents were signed, and the *Cape Ann* was renamed *Seminole.* She was purchased for conversion to an ocean-going towboat, and was to be used in the trade between Martinique and France, towing two 3,000-ton barges. She was towed to New York. Her aft deckhouse was leveled almost up as far as the stack so that a huge towing winch and bitts could be placed nearly "midship." She disappeared from Lloyd's register in 1926. The officers of the *Cape Ann* at the end were Captain Henry M. Godfrey, First Mate Leo Campbell, Chief Engineer Eugene Connolly, and Oiler William J. Sutherland.

I would like to give a quick word about the crew of the company. Captain Henry Godfrey, master of the *Cape Ann*, passed away in April 1926, in Snug Harbor, New York. He was a native of Lubec, Maine, and as you can see in the picture I have included of him, he looks every bit the part of a captain. He was 78 years old at the time. He was also the keeper of the West Quoddy Light in Maine. His first command was captain of the *George*

A. Chaffee, and for a time, he skippered the *City of Gloucester*. He ended his 22 years of service with the company on the *Cape Ann*.

William J. Sutherland joined the Boston & Gloucester Steamship Co. in 1910, first as oiler on the *Cape Ann* and then as assistant engineer on the *City of Gloucester*.

In 1924, after receiving his engineer's license, the Mariners' Towboat Co. employed him. He took a position as chief engineer and later, as a company stockholder on the steam tug *Eveleth*. This position lasted until 1937. In that year, the idle steam tug *Mariner* was converted to diesel, and the *Eveleth* was sold to John Forward, a marine contractor in Providence, Rhode Island. My father's career as a marine steam engineer came to an end, and another career as a diesel engineer began. When Loren A. Jacobs, the captain of the towboat *Mariner*, passed away in 1944, my father took on yet another new title: captain. This role lasted until June 19, 1948, when the *Mariner* was sold and the Mariners' Towboat Co. ceased to exist. My father passed away in 1970 at the age of 86. He was a native of New Brunswick, Canada, and was naturalized as an American citizen on January 3, 1916.

Edgar Merchant, who started with Mariners' as a clerk, worked his way up to become the agent for the Boston & Gloucester Steamship Co. until 1925. He was a native of Gloucester and passed away on February 2, 1928, at the age of 72.

After the *Cape Ann* was sold, it was believed that Chief Connolly shipped out on one of the three Eastern Steamship Lines steamers in their run from Boston to Nova Scotia. He said that an opening on his steamer for an assistant engineer was available and offered it to my dad if he wanted it. The position of assistant engineer on one of those liners would have provided a quantum increase in salary. I believe my mother nixed that because he would never be at home.

Charles Bumpus, the chief of the *City of Gloucester*, was a resident of Somerville. His whereabouts after the sale of the *City* are unknown. Licensed engineers could always find employment; in most cases, your reputation preceded you, and with the proper recommendations, there would be little trouble finding work. Without a doubt, Bumpus found a position on one of the many steamers that sailed out of Boston.

In the early 1900s, while the *Cape Ann* and the *City of Gloucester* were doing their thing, other companies were stirring around looking for more fertile fields. Competition arose briefly in 1902 and through the season of 1903, when an opposing line ran the new

Opposite, above left: Captain Henry Godfrey (1895–1917) of the S.S. *Cape Ann*. *J.L. Sutherland*.

Opposite, above right: W.J. Sutherland, assistant engineer and oiler on the S.S. *Cape Ann* from 1910 to 1917, shown here on the tug *Mariner*. *J.L. Sutherland*.

Opposite, below left: Eugene Connolly, chief engineer on the S.S. *Cape Ann* from 1902 to 1917. *J.L. Sutherland*.

Opposite, below right: Charles Bumpus, chief engineer on the *City of Gloucester* from 1917 to 1926. *J.L. Sutherland*

steamer by the name of *City of Haverhill* on an abbreviated schedule from Boston to Salem and Gloucester. Built in East Boston in 1902 by Robert F. Keough for the Haverhill, Newburyport & Boston Steamboat Co., she measured 121 x 24 x 10.7 feet and weighed 343 gross tons. Eventually, the steamer was to serve the ports on the Merrimack River and Boston, but after only 40 or so trips, the steamer was sold to John McKinnon of Boston for $12,000, a bargain price, renamed *Mildred*, and ran out of Providence. She was lost on a run between Florida and Cuba.

Someone once said, "Once the political bug bites you, it's hard to quit." The old adage is also true for the running of a steamship line. In 1923, the directors of the Boston & Gloucester Steamship Co., chaired by David W. Simpson, purchased the iron-hulled steamer *Mascotte*, the Plant Line's first vessel for service between Tampa, Key West, and Havana. The Peninsular, as well as the Occidental Steamship Co., operated her for 38 years. William Cramp & Sons, of Philadelphia, built the *Mascotte* in 1885 for H.B. Plant. Her specifics were as follows: official number 91818; 207 feet in length; 30 feet in breadth; 19.6 feet in depth; 884 gross tons—quite a large ship for the North Shore run. She had a steel hull and maintained a speed of 17 knots. She arrived in Gloucester on May 7, 1924, for her face lifting, and her first trip took place on July 4. The agent for the Plant Line at that time was Roderick McDonald, who was also a shipping commissioner and resided at 8 Washington Square in Gloucester. The *Mascotte*'s run to Boston was for the 1924–1925 summer months only, and the last trip was on September 30, 1925. She was reported as "abandoned" in 1930; most probably she went to the ship breakers. The last sailing of the *Mascotte* heralded the end of the Boston & Gloucester Steamship Co. From 1869 until 1925, this company was in the forefront of steamship companies on the North Shore. Early in December 1926, the Boston & Gloucester Steamship Company officially ceased to exist with the sale of the wharf and sheds on Pierce Street to the new Massachusetts Bay Steamship Co.

The officers of the Boston & Gloucester Steamship Company at the time of the sale were as follows: David W. Simpson (president and treasurer); and Frank C. Pierce, Charles F. Wonson (better known as Charlie Fred), and Fred E. Morris (directors). There was talk of the purchase of a new steamer, but with the combination of trains and the automobile, the future of excursion and freight vessels both on the North and South Shores was slowly wending its way into oblivion.

The final straw came shortly thereafter. On December 18, 1926, a few weeks after the sale of the wharf, a fire broke out in the company's storage shed. It was about seven in the morning when the first of three alarms was sounded. I was close to four years old at the time of the fire, and my family lived at 86 East Main Street in East Gloucester, directly across the street from the Slade Gorton's office.

The morning of the fire, my brothers, Bill and Allen, and I climbed the attic steps, and I can recall watching the fire from the skylight. Sparks and smoke were flying in the direction of East Gloucester and over Base 7, the old coast guard station at the far end of Barbary Shore. The next edition of the *Gloucester Daily Times* mentioned that there were some small fires started in the East Gloucester neighborhood, but they were quickly extinguished.

A faulty chimney was the attributed cause, for a small fire was started in the same area a few days before. The shed and its contents were a total loss. Damage was estimated in the vicinity of $50,000, a considerable sum in those days. In retrospect, it was fortunate that only the wharf end comprising most of the commercial storage shed was destroyed. The main two-and-a-half-story connecting building was saved, and several years later, it housed the M. Cooney Sail Co., Inc. However, with the introduction of diesel power for the many fishing vessels, the sail-making business slowly diminished to the point that producing awnings for storefronts and a few residences was the principal source of income. The final use of the building was a vessel provision store for the Sherman B. Ruth Co., and later John J. Burke took over the company.

At the time of the fire, my father was working as chief engineer on the *Eveleth*, and after the fire, some of the remaining canned goods stored there that were to be delivered to local stores were there for the taking. Our family had no end of canned mackerel, sardines, and herring in mustard sauce. Small green bottles of peppercorns were great for gifts for visitors at the cottage in West Gloucester. There were old washtubs filled with the loot, stashed under the back porch. My father picked up a few odd high-cut boots, for the leather was good for gaskets and garden hose washers.

As a side note, the tug *Mariner* towed the new 86-foot yacht *Faith*, owned by Walden Shaw of Chicago, to another pier and to safety from the fire. She was a ketch and was

B & G Steamship Co. freight sheds at steamboat wharf in Gloucester, *c.* 1926. *J.L. Sutherland.*

launched on November 3, 1926, about a month earlier at the A.D. Story yards in Essex. I have no idea where the *Eveleth* was at the time of the fire, most probably moving other endangered vessels to safer moorings. It was my father's practice to be aboard the tug very early every day ready for the day's business.

The offices of the Marines' Towboat Co. and the steamship company were completely destroyed. However, the "books" of the towboat company, dating back to 1924, are in my possession, so all was not lost. Who saved the journals and how has never been brought to light. It raises the question of what ever happened to the journals of the previous years. I wish they could have been made available; much of the day-to-day work habits could be revealed from them. I suppose they could have been destroyed when the company was reorganized in the early twenties.

As an aside, it was noted in the *Gloucester Daily Times* that at the time, and merely as a coincidence, a water break at Pierce Street prohibited the use of a hydrant nearest the fire.

There were a few other steamers that tried to make a go at the freight and passenger run from Boston to Gloucester. The 142-foot *Roseway*, launched at the Arthur D. Story yard in Essex on July 18, 1918, as a steam trawler, was converted in the spring of 1925 to a motorized freight boat. It didn't last long, and its end is not known. In March 1926, the Massachusetts Bay Steamship Co. commenced freight service between Boston, Gloucester, and Provincetown, making daily trips with the motor vessel *Governor Prence*,

Captain William J. Sutherland in the wheelhouse of the tug *Mariner* in Salem, 1946. *J.L. Sutherland.*

a converted submarine chaser. She was built in Kingston, New York, in 1917. Her official number was 224952, and she had a tonnage of 83; her measurements were 104.3 x 15.0 x 8.1 feet. The officers of this company were Joseph C. Nowell (president), E.P.A. Simpson (vice president), and Ralph C. Emery (treasurer).

On July 26, 1926, the line placed the steamer *Monhegan* in daily service between Boston and Gloucester. Captain George Steele, who in 1925 was skipper of the *Peary* on a trip to the Arctic region, commanded this vessel. The schedule for the *Monhegan* was as follows: leave Boston at 10:30 a.m.; arrive at Gloucester at 1:15 p.m. The vessel left Gloucester at 4:00 p.m. and arrived at her Atlantic Avenue pier at 6:30 p.m. Her docking pier in Gloucester was at the Charles M. Mattlage and Sons wharf at the end of Duncan Street (known locally as the "Halibut Wharf"). That wharf is long gone. The coast guard purchased the property, and they are now quartered there. This was the berth of departure of the Massachusetts Bay Steamship Co. until the old Benjamin Low wharf off Pierce Street was purchased. The losses resulting from the fire could not be overcome and the line later went bankrupt.

On January 3, 1927, the *Monhegan* made her last trip. The company was in such bad shape that the seamen were not paid wages and bills from supply firms such as the Maritime Coaling Company of Boston went unpaid. While working the Narragansett Bay area, she was wrecked at her dock in Providence by the 1938 hurricane.

Steamboat wharf in Gloucester Harbor. *Gloucester Daily Times.*

In 1931, the *Myrtle II* arrived in Gloucester at 1:00 p.m. and stayed for three hours while the passengers explored the wharves and streets of town. This steamer was built in 1901 in Boston by the William McKie shipyards. Her official number was 130934; her measurements were 151.9 x 28.1 x 11.8 feet and she had 503 gross tonnage. After a short span of trips, the service was discontinued. She was originally named *New Shoreham* and later the *Priscilla Alden.* (Her active service history included the Block Island Line, 1901–1929; Excursion Service, Boston Harbor, 1935; Boston to Plymouth, 1935; Bridgeport to Port Jefferson, 1940; and dismantled at some unknown port in 1955.)

It was sometime in late September 1949, when the Wilson Lines motor ship *Boston Belle* came to Gloucester on an excursion trip. She steamed slowly into the inner harbor and then into Smith's Cove in East Gloucester. She berthed at the Studio Restaurant's float for a few hours, and her several hundred passengers enjoyed a meal at the many establishments. Having then dined, the people wandered about the artist colony until it was time to leave. This, then, was the final visit of the excursion ships to come to Gloucester.

There must be people living today who have fond memories of the steamboat days on the North Shore. Some may even recall the rides they had on the *Cape Ann* and the *City of Gloucester* or even one or two of the later steamers that plied the waters north of Boston.

This little sojourn through the years before and after the turn of the century just might arouse some of those long forgotten memories of when, in the early morning hours, the sound of horses' hooves and the iron-wheeled jiggers clattering on the cobblestone streets were heard as goods were delivered to the steamboats. One might even wish it could all come back, if only for a little while.

TOWING AND OTHER MISCELLANY

5

With the background of this review firmly in place, let me continue to explain in greater detail not only what I personally observed and participated in, but also what was related to me by one of the principals, my father, during the early 1900s.

Most historical memoirs start at what is usually considered the beginning of the subject to be discussed. In this instance, an exception will be made.

The last tow recorded for posterity was by the converted diesel tug *Mariner* on Thursday, September 25, 1947. It was accompanying the vessel *Newton*—Ruth's to Rocky Neck Railways. The *Newton* had a rather short but quite successful career. She was built by A.D. Story and launched in Essex on September 10, 1930, for the Judy and Jeff Trawling Co. Her length was 115 feet, breadth 23 feet, and depth 11 feet; she had a 450-horsepower Fairbanks Morse (F.M.) engine, with a smaller F.M. for an electric winch drive, placed in front of the main engine. Just what was the final chapter in the career of this vessel is unknown to me at this time. Perhaps some elder fisherman has this information, but it is enough to say that she is long gone.

These few chapters will only touch on a small part of the towboat activities that started in 1869, when the first towboat of record took its place in Gloucester's history. Captain Nicholas Gangloff launched the *B.B. Gangloff* in Vincent Cove. This tug offered water as well as the service of towing of vessels. Gangloff's office was located at the Dennis and Ayer's wharf at the foot of Pierce Street. Recorded in the city directory of 1882–1883 was one Nicholas Gangloff. He had a saloon at 16 Water Street in Gloucester. Evidently towboating didn't agree with him. He also lived on the premises, close to his work.

What followed the *B.B. Gangloff* were all manner of tugs to service the fleet. Early records are scarce, but from the 1900s on, the number of tugs increased up until the 1920s. I wish only to review in some depth the period relating to towboating from the twenties

The tug *Mariner* alongside *Holy Family* on July 22, 1944. *J.L. Sutherland.*

until the inevitable end approached. I only played a minuscule part in it.

No doubt there are many anecdotes that could be offered by others that lived in the days long before my time. It is fitting that at the age of 81, the time has arrived to reflect and record on paper my views as they relate to the activities of a youngster, and later as an employee of the towboat company.

I have in my possession the Mariners' Towboat Company books dating only as far back as 1924, and it lists at that time those receiving monthly wages as follows:

A.E. Jacobs (captain)	$160.00
W.J. Sutherland (engineer)	$136.00
L.A. Jacobs (mate)	$88.00
James Corcoran (fireman)	$88.00

This was for the month of January for those working on the tug *Eveleth.* There is no mention of the tug *Priscilla* or *Nellie*—in all probability, they had been sold at that time. Jennie H. Nelson was still the bookkeeper, and some of her writing and figures are atrocious. There is no explanation of why Miss Nelson was replaced in December 1925; perhaps she just retired.

To revisit the early days, one has to note the major stockholders of the company, and if I can read the notations correctly, this is the list:

B. Payson	20 shares at $5 per share
Alfred Johnson (master mariner)	20 shares
George H. Pepples (master mariner)	19 shares
Elroy Prior (master mariner)	19 shares
Peter Grant (master mariner)	19 shares
John McKinnon (master mariner)	19 shares
Andrew E. Jacobs (captain of Eveleth)	19 shares
J.H. Nelson (secretary)	5 shares
M.F. Foley (customs inspector)	19 shares

This is referred to as "capital stock," and if any of the paper exists today, it is worthless money wise, only good for nostalgia.

Reverting back through the years, and in reviewing the Gloucester directory of 1902, it lists the following under "Towboats": *Eveleth*, Andrew E. Jacobs, captain, address: 10 Essex Avenue; *Joe Call*, Walter Smith, captain, no address given; *Priscilla*, Charles T. Heberle, captain, address: 6 Commonwealth Avenue; and *Nellie*, Osborne P. Linnekin, captain, address: 12 Lookout Street. It must be said that towboat captains and their crews, like the captains and crews of the various fishing vessels, sometimes on a whim, changed positions or retired as the times warranted. Their addresses were subject to just as many changes, mostly reflecting their financial status.

The *St. Rita*, (later *Grace F.*) with the tug *Eveleth* on March 13, 1932. *Dana Story.*

These tugs all berthed at one time or another at the steamboat wharf, located at the foot of Duncan Street. This pier was the original landing spot and remained so for many years. In the next move, the steamers *Cape Ann*, the *City of Gloucester*, and the tugs relocated to the former Benjamin Low wharf at the foot of Pierce and Wharf Streets. The Low wharf was farther into the inner harbor, and the southwest swells had much less effect on the vessels when moored there.

According to the company's journal, dated November 20, 1925, the Gloucester Towboat Co. ceased to exist. It was around this time that the tugs *Priscilla* and *Nellie* must have been sold. The sales of the *Eveleth* and the *Mariner* were negotiated through the Gloucester Safe Deposit & Trust Co., Andrew E. Jacobs (agent?), and on November 30, 1925, a new list of capital stockholders appeared as follows:

Elizabeth F. Foley	$500
Andrew E. Jacobs	$500
Wm. J. Sutherland	$500
Peter Grant	$500
Loren A. Jacobs	$500

Also on November 30, 1925, the Master Mariners' Towboat Co. came into being, with little or no fanfare. This company continued in business under this title until it dissolved in 1947. The last of the regular commercial towing services in Gloucester came to a halt. On June 19, 1948, the tug *Mariner* was sold at auction for $4,500. The vast majority of the early information imparted in this narrative came from the journals of the company from January 1924 until September 1947 and firsthand information gleaned from my father.

After 24 years with the Mariners' Towboat Co., Captain William J. Sutherland, member of the corporation, dropped the anchor and retired to a life on dry land. This after 14 years with the Boston & Gloucester Steamship Co. (seven years as oiler on the steamer *Cape Ann*, for a few years assistant engineer on the *City of Gloucester*); then as chief engineer and stockholder on the steam tug *Eveleth*; diesel engineer and finally captain of the tug *Mariner*. From 1910 on, steam engineering was a way of life, but in retirement, there were other fields of endeavor to cultivate. Now ashore, his marine certificate would not be valid to operate a stationary engine, so he applied to the State Department of Public Safety for the proper license. Using his marine license as proof of experience, my father was issued a third class stationary engineers certificate #1611 on November 17, 1948, enough to operate any steam plant in the city of Gloucester. Later, a renewal license, # 1779, was issued, good until November 17, 1951.

As he had no further use of the marine license, my father surrendered it when he received the stationary steam license. Marine certificates were, and are, very ornate. It would have been nice to have in my possession, but it was not meant to be.

My father's first job ashore was at Burnham's railway as stationary steam engineer, running a "Brown" engine. That position lasted until a fire ravished the boiler and engine

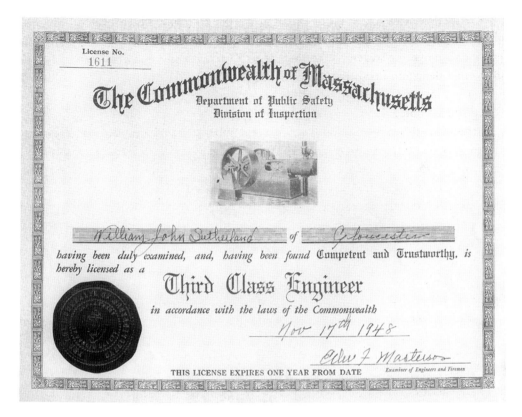

Above: William J. Sutherland's
Third Class Engineer's License.
J.L. Sutherland.

Right: Renewal License for
Third Class Engineer William
J. Sutherland. *J.L. Sutherland*.

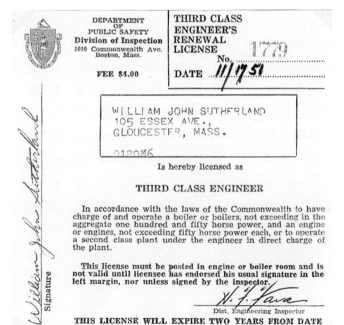

room. The hauling tracks were then electrified, and the services of an engineer were no longer needed. For a short while after that, my dad was the engineer at the Cape Ann Laundry on Parker Street. That establishment eventually went out of business, and thus ended his professional career.

The Mariners' Towboat Co. record books contain information, dates, names of vessels, fees for towing, etc., and reference is made here to it quite often. In my research from 1936, when I was part-time on deck of the *Mariner*, to nearly the time I entered the service on January 19,1942, I was present for four launchings at Ipswich and eight at Essex.

The Mariners' Towboat Co. did not get all the towing jobs out of Essex; the *Betsy Ross*, a small steam tug, of the Ross Towboat Co. of Boston had a few. How that company could send a tug all the way from Boston to Essex and return to Boston with a vessel, and do it cheaper than the local company, always amazed me.

I observed several Ipswich vessel launchings when I was a deckhand on the tug *Mariner*; they were the yacht *Swift* (May 28, 1938), *Lady of Good Voyage* (November 28, 1940), *Niantic* (April 24, 1940), and the *Thomas Lawrence* (September 12, 1939). This is not counting the many army and navy tugs that were launched at that yard during the war years.

Monthly receipts from January 1926, for the Mariners' Towboat Company of Gloucester. *J.L. Sutherland.*

The Ipswich yard came into being around 1938, with the idea of building historic vessels. William A. Robinson, with the aid of the noted marine author and writer Howard I. Chapelle, established the yard in a backwater of the Ipswich River, called Fox Creek. It was a winding creek with a sandbar every boat length, and if there ever was a tougher place to get to, I'll wager it would be hard to find. It could only be navigated on the highest of tides. Dredging was done periodically. William had married Florence Crane, the daughter of the plumbing mogul, and the area was part of her estate. Ms. Crane was the principal financier of the project.

The *Swift* was the first of many of the diverse hulls to be launched there. The last could have been the steel-hulled *Captain Dave*, an oil boat to be located in Gloucester. It was to take the place of the aging wooden double ender, *Mayflower*. Among the most notable was the brigantine *Florence C. Robinson*, known as the *Yacht*, skippered by Sterling Hayden, adventurer, actor, and seaman extraordinaire. After the maiden voyage to Tahiti in the fall of 1938, Hayden sailed with the crew of the Gloucester schooner *Gertrude L. Thebaud*, during the fishermen's races in 1938. I had the pleasure of making Hayden's acquaintance in his later years.

Before WWII, when I was a hand on the tug *Mariner*, I observed the launchings of the *Yacht, Swift, Lady of Good Voyage, Thomas D.,* and the *Thomas Lawrence*. After 1941, WWII came and shipbuilding was greatly expanded. Countless army yard tugs (Y.T.'s)

The otter trawler *Louis A. Thebaud* and tug *Eveleth* on April 3, 1930. *Dana Story.*

The schooner *Gertrude L. Thebaud* and tug *Eveleth* on March 17, 1930. *Dana Story.*

were built and launched there. After launching, the tugs' hulls were towed to Gloucester, to what is now the Beacon Marine Basin, to be fitted out. Shortly after the war, the ship-yard was phased out.

The Essex launchings were *St. Anthony* (October 5, 1940), *Governor Saltonstall* (April 20, 1940), *Manual Roderick* (March 4, 1941), *Skillogollee* (May 1, 1938), *Jean and Ursler* (August 7, 1937), *Ronald and Mary Jane* (September 4, 1941), and the *Theresa Boudreau* (November 20, 1941). (Between January 19, 1942, and November 17, 1945, I was in the service.)

After my separation from the service, and in less than two or three weeks, I was hi-jacked, in a manner of speaking, by my father to go as an engineer on the *Mariner*. I had seen my father operate the Fairbanks Morse engine many times, but watching and doing are two different things. Nothing to it, says he. "All you gotta to do is listen for the bells and turn this wheel this-a-way or that-a-way and give the throttle what it needs." So much for instructions—it took a while to catch on, but in a day or two, I had it down so as not to cause any real harm.

From December 1945, until the sale of the *Mariner* on June 19, 1948, there were ten fishing vessels launched in Essex that the company was hired for the tow to Gloucester. The names and the dates of launching were as follows: *Julie Ann* (May 6, 1946), *Benjamin C.* (June 27, 1946), *St. Nicholas* (November 9, 1946), *Famigilia* (March 23, 1947), *Kingfisher* (March 25, 1947), *Mother Ann* (April 4, 1947), *Bright Star* (April 9, 1947), *St. Rosalie* (July 10, 1947), *Mary and Josephine* (August 22, 1947), and the *Salvatore and*

The *St. Nicholas* on November 9, 1946. *J.L. Sutherland.*

Grace (September 13, 1947). There were three other vessels launched that should be mentioned here. Two of them were the *Nancy* (launched in Friendship, Maine, on March 21, 1941) and the *Gloucester* (launched in Kennebunkport, Maine, on August 29, 1941); both were towed to Gloucester. The *Andrew and Rosalie* was built and launched from Sherman Ruth's wharf.

During the past 65 years, there has been many a tale going around about how the *Henry Ford* happened to go on the beach while being towed out of the Essex River. Everyone has his or her own version of what really did happen that day. My father, in chatting with Captain Andrew Jacobs of the *Eveleth* (Father was not on the towboat at this time), gave this version of the events.

First of all, it must be said that as the towboats *Eveleth* and *Lebanon H. Jenkens* were cleared of any fault in the mishap, there must be a modicum of truth as to this version of the events on that momentous occasion. On April 11, 1922, the year I was born, the *Ford* was launched in Essex at the Story yard. There is always a celebration of sorts when a new vessel at any of the yards gets wet, and that there was plenty of "Dugan's Dew" sloshing around was no secret.

Because of an exceptionally swift launching, the *Ford* sailed down the ways in good style. The dunnage and chains that were to slow her sternway evidently were less than enough and she grounded stern first, without damage, into what was then the marshy island a short distance away. This necessitated some working of the vessel to free her, and it took both tugs a good part of an hour to accomplish this. All launchings, as in this case,

Gloucester tug *Eveleth* at Ruth's Wharf in 1937. *J.L. Sutherland.*

Old postcard print of Gloucester Harbor. *J.L. Sutherland.*

are scheduled to take place as near high tide as possible. This was so new vessels would not take bottom, with ensuing damage to the rudder and shoe. It is most important that any vessel get out of the Essex River and across the bar and into Ipswich Bay as soon as possible. In this case, with the hour delay, time was of the essence. Like all big schooners, which tend to draw anywhere from 10 to 14 feet, the *Ford* drew 12 feet, and it would be nip and tuck to clear the bar.

I must say that it was not unusual to lay the newly launched vessel alongside the pier closest to the causeway and near the small bridge called "Corporation Wharf." This enabled the public a close-up view of the new addition to the Gloucester fleet. It was also not unusual for a number of hardy souls to come aboard a vessel and take the trip to Gloucester.

In the case of the *Ford's* launching, there was no mention of the number of "passengers" this day, or even if the vessel berthed at the pier. For whatever reason, when it was time to get underway, some of the tide had slipped away.

Perhaps in hindsight, it would have been in the best interest of all to lay over another day. There is some evidence that the contract agreed to by Mr. Story and Captain Clayton Morrissey stated that the vessel was to be delivered in Gloucester and only then could Mr. Story collect the $30,000 due. In the twenties, this sum of money could mean the difference between a healthy business or going under. The technical owner of the *Ford* was the builder, and it was only with his acquiescence that the tow was made.

Captain Andrew Jacobs (or "Jake," as he was called) related that everything went smoothly until crossing the Essex River sand bar, where, in a slight ground swell, the vessel fetched up and in the extra strain needed to get her free, the tow lines parted. In the narrow confines of the channel, it was impossible to secure another hawser without putting the tugs in danger of grounding. The vessel, under the influence of what little wind and tide there was, turned broadside in the narrow channel and was on her own. The river's mouth just off of the Hawk's estate had great numbers of ledges and rocks of all description. Lady Luck played out her hand, and the vessel was stranded on sand, with few apparent damages.

The next tide was somewhere near 11:30 p.m., and night work in that area was out of the question. During the night, the wind increased somewhat from the east and drove the *Ford* farther up on the beach. She rested on her port side, and only on the sand.

The *Henry Ford*, after five days on the beach, was freed and arrived in Gloucester on Easter Sunday, but not without the efforts of several tugs and a lighter. There was some damage to the vessel, a few planks, some of the "shoe," and some caulking. The towboat company swallowed the cost of the towing from the launching to the site of the mishap. Negligence on the part of the tugs was asserted but never to the point of a lawsuit.

The *Ford* was finally delivered in Gloucester some five days later by the tug *Neptune*, out of Boston. As was previously stated, the *Henry Ford* was built on the order of Captain Clayton Morrissey, and the agreement stated that the vessel was to be delivered in Gloucester, and payment rendered. As the mishap happened while under Mr. Story's care,

The diesel tug *Mariner* off Ruth's Wharf in Gloucester in 1938. The new freezer on Fish Pier on Five Pound Island can be seen in the distance. *J.L. Sutherland.*

A view of Gloucester Harbor *c.* 1900. *J.L. Sutherland.*

there was some dickering about "damaged goods" and demands that some adjustment in cost should be made. How that was worked out rested with the two principals. The January 21, 1924 entry of the Master Mariners' Towboat Co. record book noted that a payment was received from "The Race Committee, $75," for services on October 21, 1923. A payment for $5 on the same day was billed to the *Henry Ford.* This must have had to do with the races of the previous year, or perhaps a harbor tow.

It is interesting to note that in the towboat "books" of January 3, 1924, the charge to tow the *B.T. Hillman* (67 feet), a typical new vessel, albeit half the size of the *Ford* (122 feet), from Essex to Gloucester was $40. Imagine hiring a tug with a four-man crew for less than $8 an hour! The bill was paid on January 24, funds of A.D. Story.

This is reminiscent of a similar situation about the festivities when the schooner *Mayflower* was launched on April 12, 1921. Any delay, for any reason, in getting underway with a deep-hulled vessel would cause concern before reaching deep water outside of the Essex bar. From the start of the launching ways until clearing the ever-threatening Essex River sandbar, it was nothing more than a glorified creek. The highest of tides were needed for any vessel with a 12-foot, or better, draft.

There was a time my father related to me about a tow coming out of Essex. The name of the newly launched vessel escapes me at the moment, but it had to get to Gloucester the same day. The *Eveleth* had the vessel under tow, and everything was going well as they were clearing the bar of Essex River. The wind had whipped up quite a chop, and as the tug heeled and rolled, low and behold, coals, grates, and all in the starboard fire box fell into the ash pit, causing an immediate 50 percent loss in steaming capacity. This would not be of concern if the tug were running free with no tow, but with only one-half of the boiler's heating output usable, it was time to get a little worried.

The boiler setup is something like this. The boiler was of the Scotch type, which is a fire tube. Heat generated passes to the back of the fire space, up and through maybe 140 two-inch tubes, to the breaching in front of the boiler and then up the stack. Below this configuration is the furnace space and below that the ash pit. This boiler had two separate furnaces with two fire doors and two ash pits. Separating the two was a steel partition that, in combination with the outer shell of the boiler, had heavy angle irons that supported the grates. Somehow, several of the grate bars, having been weakened by constant heat, broke, spilling the fire into the pit.

My brother Roy was the fireman at the time, and it was decided that the grates be reset, while firing the other side of the furnace. Now this is not the best of jobs. First, you have to clear the furnace area of all coals. Then, hose down the cinders in the ash pit so there are no hot embers to deal with and rake the ashes out. Next, cool the remaining good grates so that someone can handle them and add new replacements. Now comes the good part. Someone has to get into the ash pit to do the work. Big Brother Roy was elected. He donned all the clothes he could, and put on over them old oil clothes. He lay down on his back, and while

Roy W. Sutherland was a fireman on the tug *Eveleth. J.L. Sutherland.*

The dragger *Carlo & Vince* and the tug *Eveleth* on February 23, 1932. *Dana Story.*

he slid into the ash pit, water was hosed on him to keep him as cool as possible while he placed several new grates on their racks. This took the best part of 20 minutes, and man-handling 80- to 90-pound grate bars at arms length over your body, with a full furnace fired up inches away, was no bed of roses. A fire hose poured seawater over you, while you slopped in three inches of hot water in the ash pit—this is not a fun time.

It was done, and a few shovels of embers from the hot furnace were admitted to the cold side, and fired up as if nothing had ever happened. Roy mentioned later that thanks were in order, but nothing extra was in the pay envelope. It was considered part of the job.

When in my teens and too young to work on the tug, I thought going to Essex was always a red-letter day for me. It was regrettable that I did not have the money to have a camera to take snapshots of the events, but these were the Depression days. I remember well the early trips on the *Eveleth*. As I was the "Chief's" son, I positioned myself on the top deck under the wheelhouse windows, which provided an unobstructed view. In the mid-thirties, during summer vacations, these were the most enjoyable of times. At age 17 or so, I was hired off and on as deckhand and viewed many vessels as they slid down the ways. Later, from time to time, from 1938 until January 1942 and my entrance in the service, I was a deckhand on the tug *Mariner*.

In the early thirties, the tug *Eveleth* was to attend a launching in Essex. Usually I made as many trips to Essex as possible, but for some reason, this was one time I couldn't make it. Father related the events as they happened. It was common practice that when about to launch a vessel, the rudder would be securely fastened in a midship position. Securing the steering wheel or perhaps fastening wooden stops to the rudder itself would serve the purpose. This was so that the vessel would follow a straight and designated path through the open water basin dead astern, and not stray into the marsh island, perhaps a couple of thousand feet beyond.

According to Murphy's Law, the unusual happens, and this time things did not go according to plan. As the stern hit the water, the rudder bracings gave way, and the vessel, its name long forgotten, veered to port. The *Eveleth* was tied to the nearest pier as she had been in the past, about at the corner where the boatyard is now. Little did anyone dream that its position would put it right in the path of a seemingly out-of-control vessel. (In Dana Story's *The Shipbuilders of Essex*, he refers to the pier as Corporation Wharf.)

As all hands scattered as the huge overhanging schooner stern crashed into the forward starboard quarter of the *Eveleth*, cleaning out several feet of rail and stanchions. Its stern ended up well into the boiler room house. It was fortunate that the main steam line did not rupture. In the future, more times than not, the tug nosed itself into the marsh well away from any rambunctious vessels to avoid a repeat of that day.

An company book entry on January 2, 1924, was the payment for towing the schooner *Radio* on December 21, 22, 24, and 31, 1923, from J.F. James & Son. This must have been for harbor towing. The *Radio* was launched from the James yard on December 8, 1923, and I have no records before January 1924, of who towed the vessel to Gloucester. There was an expense of $20.12 on January 7 for food at the "Model Market," probably on Main Street. It had to be for a meal for the crew away on some job. The balance in the book for January 1924, was $4,399.

The tug *Eveleth*'s crew at that time was Captain Andrew E. Jacobs, Chief Engineer William J. Sutherland, Mate Loren A. Jacobs, and James Corcoran (listed in the 1928 assessor's return as an engineer). Corcoran probably was the fireman at the time, getting experience to sit for his license. Speaking of Corcoran, my father told of a humorous event when the *Eveleth* was towing the *Mariner* to Boston for the annual marine inspection at the Hodge Boiler Works in East Boston.

The *Mariner* was not allowed to go to Boston under her own power, but it would help if Corcoran could get some steam up, and with its engine turning over, make the tow easier. Just about at Half Way Rock, Captain Jacobs, in the *Eveleth*, noticed that they weren't making much headway. Looking back, he observed that Corcoran had the *Mariner*'s engine in reverse. Andy whistled for attention, and after some hand signals, and a lot of mean-spirited words, Corcoran got the message, and threw the links to "ahead." Both tugs then continued on without further trouble.

When the towboats moved to the Low wharf, the Duncan Street location eventually became the Gloucester Gaslight Company property, where illuminating gas was manufactured. The office was located on Water Street.

By this time, the tug *Nellie* had been sold, and it came to me from a fairly reliable source that it ended up as the *Gorham H. Whitney*. The owner was the Bay State Dredging Co.

Steam tugs *Eveleth* and *Nellie* of Mariners' Towboat Company, berthed in Gloucester in 1920. The location is now the Americold Pier. *Gloucester Daily Times.*

Records are not available, but it is conceivable that it was the *Priscilla* that was later named the *Gorham H. Whitney*, for having seen her many times towing scows, it looked somewhat larger than the *Nellie*. Whatever happened to the *Whitney* since last seen by me in the late 1940s is anybody's guess. The *Priscilla*'s tonnage was around 46, and she was about five feet longer than the *Nellie*; the tonnage of the *Nellie* was about 31.

So here we only have the tugs *Mariner* and *Eveleth* to continue on. Even though the *Eveleth* was older, she was the pet of the two tugs, more because she was fitted with a condenser, and with the great saving of fresh water, she could do outside towing. The *Mariner*, on the other hand, exhausted into the atmosphere, and fresh water had to be available to service the boiler. The *Eveleth* and the *Mariner* had the same engines and were powered to handle the vessels in and around the Gloucester area. Most of the small 60-foot tugs were equipped with Bertlesen & Petersen steam engines—they were considered "standard" for harbor tugs.

Quoting from Dana Story in the *The Shipbuilders of Essex*, "on June 6, 1907, the tug *Mariner* was launched by Tarr & James in Essex; the bare hull cost was $3,500. A few days later she was towed to the Hodge boiler works at East Boston where an engine and the boiler were installed. On July 31, she was in active service in Gloucester."

The boiler was an "upright"; that is, the shell was cylindrical and the fire grates were directly under the open ends of the tubes, with a conical affair on top to connect to the stack. Two doors, set about four feet apart, and carrying 175 to 200 psi of pressure, fired

The tug *Mariner* prior to making a trip to New York in 1947. The *Mariner* was built in 1907 by James & Tarr of Essex. *J.L. Sutherland.*

it. The Bertlesen & Petersen Engine Works of Philadelphia built the engine. The engine was a single-cylinder, double-acting affair. Steam would be admitted on the top and bottom of the cylinder, giving the engine two power strokes per revolution. If I remember correctly, the piston was around 20 inches; with a stroke of about 26 inches, it turned a four-bladed cast-iron propeller of about 60 inches in diameter at 130 to 140 rpms. When pushed, another 10 rpms could be nursed out. (Father told me the exact bore and stroke of the engine, but age has taken its toll; the figures are within an acceptable range.)

The *Mariner* had an atmospheric exhaust system and used a lot of fresh water; a 3,000-gallon tank was located in the forward quarter of the hull. On rare occasions, because of low power, the *Mariner* would be used on a short easy outside tow, but care had to be taken not to run low on water. In a pinch, saltwater could be used, but should be avoided if at all possible because of the frothing in the boiler and carryover to the engine. The exhaust from these engines would be visible at the smokestack as a "chuf chuf" cloud of vapor.

The tug *Eveleth* had the same size and type of engine, which was built by the same company, except that it utilized a two-cylinder, double-acting Worthington steam pump to circulate cool saltwater through a steam condenser. This system allowed the expended steam to revert back into water. This water then would be drained into a so-called "hot well." With only a little make-up water to be added, it would be injected back into the boiler, and the process was repeated over and over again. The addition of a condenser al-

Steam tugs *Eveleth* and *Mariner* at Ruth's Wharf in Gloucester in 1932. The fishing vessel *Claudia* can be seen in the foreground and Five Pound Island is in the distance. *J.L. Sutherland.*

lowed the tug to make extended tows outside the harbor, only to be governed by the coal reserves. For a boiler feed apparatus, a "Hancock" inspirator and a "Penberthy" injector were available. By marine law, two means of boiler feed were mandatory.

Both the *Eveleth's* and the *Mariner's* engines were operated at deck level, the fire room below, on a steel-plated deck. The doors on deck, and a small skylight provided the only ventilation. On hot days, with steam up, it was quite uncomfortable, but with only a few steps, one could be on deck for some relief.

Now, with the *Eveleth* as the chief outside-the-harbor tug, it was in the works to get a larger engine. It would have been costly to purchase a compound, or two-cylinder engine, plus the whole bed would have to be extended forward, which would restrict the fireman in his duties. It was undesirable to undertake this plan of action. The next best thing to double the horsepower was to "steeple" the engine, meaning only to put another cylinder on top of the present engine, going up, not forward on the base. In the account book, a pair of four-bladed cast-iron wheels was ordered through the Reed Foundry on Maplewood Avenue. This gave new power, but it did not overcome the inherent flaw of single crank engines—getting stuck on top or bottom center. I can just hear the old man muttering under his breath at it, finally having to tell the fireman down below to bar it over, and all this when bearing down on a dock or into another vessel.

When the engine had to be bared off of centers, steam would have to be cut off; otherwise, with the bar still engaged in the jacking gear holes of the small flywheel, the engine would take off and the bar would be sent flying. It caused many an anxious moment. It didn't happen often because one could look down through the grating and throw the links at the right time. Reversing the engine on the last stroke cushions the pistons, preventing them from descending all the way. "Steepling" the engine, putting one cylinder on top of another, only made it a "double acting, double simple" engine (i.e., steam would be admitted alternately to the same ends of the two cylinders at the same time, but was used only once and was then exhausted and condensed). It roughly doubled the horsepower, but was not as economical as a compound engine would be. With the additional height, the engine could still be easily operated at deck level, giving the chief a view of what was happening. Many are the times I sat and watched the piston rod in its almost hypnotizing endless up and down motion, wondering all the time what made it do that.

The maker's nameplate, "Bertlesen and Petersen," adorned the rear bulkhead of the *Eveleth's* engine room along with a set of steam pressure and vacuum gauges, as well as a matching pair located close to the boiler. There was also a Seth Thomas clock, with chimes, which could be heard clearly above the gentle hissing of the plant. A skylight gave light as well as ventilation. On the deck-level engine-operating space, there was a long narrow bench fitted against the boiler room bulkhead. It had lift-up covers and held the tools needed to service the engine. Another toolbox for the many small wrenches was also handy.

When the steam pressure dropped slightly, there was a round "head-hole" in the bulkhead, and Father would poke his head through it and get on the fireman's rump to stoke it up. Getting rid of the ashes was a problem, for it was not the practice to just dump them over the side wherever you happened to be. The ashes piled up on the furnace room floor, and the time to clean house occurred every day or two on a regular run to Salem or Beverly to dock a barge.

The fireman would hook up a woven wood basket to a pulley, fill the basket, and the chief on deck would hoist it up and over the side it would go. Usually, it would amount to about 15 to 18 baskets. Then, of course, with all that dust flying around, it was hose-down time. When all finished, the tug would be about abeam of Gales Ledge buoy off Manchester.

The most reliable fireman that was employed by the company when I was a kid was Albert Caston. Before that, Morrell Jacobs and my brother Roy Sutherland had a hand at it. Morrell left and went to Boston Towboat Co. as engineer on the *Hercules*. Roy went to the Cape Ann Tool Co. in Rockport.

The noises and smells that were associated with the firing of the furnace are not easily forgotten. Every time the doors were opened hot gasses from the half-burned coal escaped from the fire. And the heat, when you were standing near the fire doors when they were opened, it felt like a thousand suns.

In the furnace, the soft coals would cake up and a slice bar would be run into clinkers and pried up, exposing the white coals beneath. After a few shovels of fresh soft coal on top, the doors were closed and a short rest for 10 to 15 minutes was most welcome. This tedious labor would be repeated hours on end.

Once in a while, on exceptionally calm days, and with a stern warning to stay clear of the fireman and engine, I would be allowed to go down below and watch in fascination the engine in its endless reciprocating motion. With every down stroke, the crosshead slipper would travel down the guide and dip into the oil cup filled with a combination of linseed oil and water. It had a yellow color to it. I'd wager there isn't a kid alive today that wouldn't jump at a chance to stand where I stood and view the same scene those many years ago. Alas, once gone, it was never to return.

When the *Eveleth* was sold in 1937, I guess Al retired. In looking at the Gloucester assessor's return of April 1, 1928, his name is not listed. This could be because he did not vote, or he wasn't around when the assessors Frank A. Rogers, Samuel Montgomery, or William A. Homans paid a visit.

I remember Al well. Of medium build, wiry, with high cheekbones—a well-put-together individual. Both of his arms were covered with tattoos, and they could be readily seen, for he had his shirtsleeves rolled up most of the time. And he smoked! He rolled his own, using "Bull Durham" in the little cloth bag with the drawstring and the Zigzag papers tucked away in the roll of his sleeve. In thinking it over and sizing this individual up, I think he was everyman's coal handler. He would grind away, hour after hour, and I can't remember him ever voicing a complaint. Oh, I suppose there must have been times when the air was blue, like if a grate bar would drop into the ash pit or when the slice bar didn't do the job, but not when I was around. Most always he had a smile or a good word. Once in a while, Dad and Al would get into it about how to fire the furnace, but cooler heads would always prevail in the long run, because Dad needed a good reliable fireman, and Al needed the job.

A few years ago, I did see and talk with him at the drop-in center here in town; he said he was living in Rockport. That's the last I have heard of him. I did inquire about him later; word was that he went to Philadelphia to live with some kinfolks. That was a while back, of course. By now, he has passed away. Years ago, Al lived at 4½ Perkins Street and was married to a lady named Evabelle. I believe they had one son.

THE *EVELETH*

The steam tug *Eveleth* was built in 1897 at Bishop's yard in Gloucester. Some 30 years later, the same boiler was producing steam. It was slowly showing its age, and leaks were

Captain Loren Jacobs (in the wheelhouse) and Engineer W.J. Sutherland (on deck) on the Gloucester tug *Eveleth* at Ruth's Wharf, *c.* 1935. *J.L. Sutherland*.

prevalent in every part of the shell. Rivet heads were a constant problem and some were totally inaccessible. Hodge Boiler Works in East Boston suggested renewing the boiler and it was taken under advisement. My brother Allen knows about that, for he spent some time "reheading" boilers as best he could. He was of slight build and could squeeze in between the boiler and the hull. Tubes would leak occasionally, so a long threaded rod and two end caps would be fitted to seal the ends. Permanent repairs would come at the annual inspection at the Hodge Boiler Works.

There were many times when vessels were to be launched from the railways after a painting or other work. The towboat would be called to stand by, and nose into the end of the pier next to the slip with the engine slow ahead; this way there was no need to tie up. When the vessel eases out of the slip, it's relatively easy to make up alongside and get underway.

Chains used to haul the cradle and vessels were the same size as today's. They were about a 14-inch link, perhaps 1 inch or 1.5 inches in heft, and weighed 40 pounds. Everyone has heard about the "weakest link." Well, it happens that once in a while chains do part and cause some anxious moments. A runaway vessel from, say Burnham's railway, could end up on the shore of Rocky Neck. When this happens, it's best to have a line ready to snare the passing vessel and make up into the stream. Most times it works out to everyone's relief.

On the lighter side, I would like to insert here something that happened when I was six or seven years old. On Sundays, it was Father's practice to go to Mass at St. Ann's Church with me in tow, and afterwards to go down to the steamboat wharf and shake up the fire. On this particular Sunday, he was wearing a brand-new straw hat, a "boater," with a wide black hatband decorated with narrow colored stripes through it. He had just purchased it from Henry the Hatter's the night before. Henry's establishment was on the corner of Porter and Main Streets.

As we approached the tug, a gull with larceny in its heart, let fly with a load of what gulls are famous for, and I'll wager that if the hat had a bull's eye on it, this gull would be the ace of the flock. My father knew that he was hit, and with a few choice words, scaled the skimmer, like a frisbee, as far as he could. Thinking about it now, it was a little humorous, but then, it was a different story. I just put my head down and took no note of what had happened.

Sometimes on the winter weekends, some of us kids would go with Dad down to the boat so he could check on the fire and water in the boiler. If there had been a particularly cold night before, gulls would perch on the rim of the stack to keep warm. Some would face into the stack and as a result, the fumes would take its effect, and the bird would tumble in and down into the damper.

My father would tip the damper, swing open the doors on the face of the tube sheet, and there would be a dead gull or two lying there. He would pick them up and fire them into the furnace, where they were consumed in no time. In the winter, this was almost a daily occurrence; there was nothing cruel about it.

In the late 1800s and early 1900s, there were upwards of eight towboats working the harbor. Competition was keen. My dad used to tell me about some of the "hairy" times before he shipped on the *Eveleth* around 1925.

Unofficial towboat rules were that the first one to get a line aboard a vessel, made fast or not, got the tow. In the race to secure first place, close calls were an everyday occurrence; and some, if it were not for the serious consequences, would be downright hilarious.

Once, Father told me about the time when Andy Jacobs was the captain of the *Eveleth*, and while racing for a tow, he misjudged the turning radius when coming alongside of a vessel. As a result, the main boom of another vessel, which had nothing to do with the vessel to be towed, came aboard just aft of the smoke stack braces and cleaned off the skylight, lantern box, lifeboat, and after mast.

Old Andrew, "Jake" or "Andy" to all who knew him, scored a point on his competitors and got, at that day and age, the $4 tow. That the effort caused about $60 in damages, a considerable sum in those days, was all taken in stride, just part of the business. If a captain wasn't aggressive, he didn't last long. On the other hand, if he was gung-ho and caused too much damage, he was replaced. Of course, if he had shares in the company, like Andy did, it was the price of doing business.

In the days of sail, bowsprits and main booms were hazards to be avoided at all costs. Another captain, while trying to squeeze between two vessels, misjudged the turn. The long bowsprit of another vessel cleaned out three windows and frames of the pilothouse on the *Mariner*, the captain ducking just in time. This kind of mischief kept a lot of ship's carpenters busy.

Gloucester tug, *Mariner*, on a harbor outing. *J.L. Sutherland.*

Andrew E. Jacobs was the captain of the *Eveleth* from well before 1902, and at the time of his death in 1930, he was 65 years of age. He was a portly gentleman. I'd say he was well into 300 pounds. I recall the times when he would come down the wharf ladder to board the tug—one step on the rail cap and the tug would take on a noticeable list.

Because Jacobs was rather portly and the wheelhouse was none too big, the *Eveleth* was fitted with a steam steerer, with the lever directly in front on the handsome inlaid wheel. To go from hard right rudder to hard left rudder was a simple push or pull of the handle. The spokes were a blur, for it took all of a second for the rudder to hit the stops. The wheel was not like today's wheel—the kind with a smooth rim all around. This one had the handgrips exposed to catch whatever was handy, and catch they did. Andy always wore a suit coat, and it was his practice to lean out a side window to observe what was happening to the tow alongside. If he wanted to shift rudder positions, the wheel was vicious and ripped the pockets to shreds. He must have been a believer in repetition, so after damaging one coat, he always changed into the raggedy coat as he entered the wheelhouse.

Jacobs was born in Norway in 1865 and died in 1930. He was married to Amanda Samual, or "Mandy" to those who knew her well. She was born in Iceland in 1866 and passed away in 1946. Early on, the family lived at 10 Essex Avenue. At the time I knew them, they lived at 5 Prospect Square. I believe they had four, maybe five children: Gladys A. (1894–1947), Loren A. (1898–1945), William Helme (1902–1975), and Morrell (1908–1974). There was also a Una R. Jacobs, born in Gloucester in 1896 and died in

Captain William J. Sutherland on the far right of the deck of tug *Mariner* before heading out to New York in 1947. *J.L. Sutherland.*

1939. This person (man or woman) may have been the second born; all are interred in Oak Grove Cemetery.

The three boys followed the sea. When Andrew died in 1930, Loren, who was married to Hazel, took over as captain of the tug *Eveleth.* He had been working as deckhand, and he fit right in. He was captain of the *Eveleth* until 1937, and then the *Mariner* until November 8, 1945, when he suffered a stroke and passed away; he was only a young 47 years of age. Bill went to the marine school in New York and served on the training ship *Nantucket.* He later decked on the tug. In later years, his heart and back gave him trouble; he retired and the last I heard lived for a time in Rockport with his wife, Marguerite, on Granite Street, and passed away there. Morrell ("Honk" was his nickname) followed his towboat career with the Boston Towboat Co. as assistant engineer on several of their

A 1946 photograph showing two of Ben Pine's vessels, the *Columbia* and the *Puritan*, with the *Mary Rose*, a typical Gloucester Trawler, in the foreground. *J.L. Sutherland.*

tugs, ending up as chief on the *Hercules*. Morrell was my father's favorite of the family and kept his friendship for many years. Morrell lived with his wife, Theresa, and passed away some years ago; his last address was in Arlington, Massachusetts.

The first mention of my brother Roy's employment on the tug was in June 1930, and he earned $9 in wages. What he did, decking or firing, is not mentioned. He continued on as a fireman until 1936 or 1937 (these are rough guesses) and went to the Cape Ann Tool Co., where he operated the largest steam hammer for some time. In 1942, he left the company to go fishing. He swung a priority and went as an engineer on many vessels, to name a few: the *Evzone*, *Leretha*, *Francis McPhearson*, *Hilda Garston*, the *Surge* and the *Surf*, two big trawlers out of Boston. There were a lot more, but these are the important ones. After some years he retired, and worked as a watchman at the old Birdseye plant on Commercial Street, until he passed away on May 19, 1984. "Hoss," as he was better known to us, had been married and divorced. He had two children, Roy Jr. and Eugene H. I think I was closest to him in later years, mostly because we were the only ones of the family in Gloucester (my other brothers lived out of town), and Natalie, my wife, and I would have him over to our house on most weekends, or perhaps go for a ride in the car. While he was watchman, he kept me in good supply of fish.

There is one incident that bears mention about Roy when he was a fireman on the *Eveleth.* The J.S. Packard Co., of Boston, was awarded the dredging contract to deepen Annisquam River. The dredging started on August 3, 1936, and ended November 3, just three months later. During that time, as the company records show, 49 of the working periods were 24-hour stretches; the other days were 12- to 14-hour periods.

Now all this time, it was mostly towing a loaded scow out to be dumped in Ipswich Bay, and then barely back in time to tow another loaded scow out. The only time the tug did something different was to coal up and get water at the Gloucester Coal Co. wharf. Steam had to be kept up, so Roy was kept busy, hour after hour, relieved once in a while by Father, so he could get his breath and perhaps a little shut-eye. Well, there was only so much of this he could take, so on one day, during a momentary lull, he took off. No one could find him. They had the cops out looking for him because he was holding up the works. They hired some temporary fireman to fill in, and in about four days he showed up. He was holed up at his girlfriend's house, sleeping most of the time. He once showed me a burn scar on his back where he has fallen asleep, standing up against the coalbunker, and slipped against a hot steam pipe. Enough was enough.

There were some good times when we sailed on the tug to Salem, Beverly, and Manchester to dock loaded barges and tow the empty ones to the anchoring grounds. Those were the times when we would eat aboard. For the short trips, there were sandwiches and tonics, lots of tonics. There was bluebird grape, orange crush, root beer, sarsaparilla, Moxie, lemon-lime, and many more. I recall the times, when seven or eight years old, when old Andy would give me some money, and send me up to what I remember as the Cloverdale store, corner of Elm and Main. At that time, in the late 1920s, it could have been the "Model Market." He would tell me to get his favorite jam—strawberry—along with bread, butter, and yellow grapes, if, and IF, they were good ones; don't come back with any wrinkled ones. "Tell the man they are for Andy Jacobs," he would say. I did, and they were the best. If there was any small change, he would let me have it. The galley on the *Eveleth* was located forward under the wheelhouse; on the *Mariner*, it was aft. There wasn't much room in the *Eveleth's* galley because the steam steering engine was located aft under a shelved partition and just forward of the boiler. The galley table faced forward and seated three persons. Bill Jacobs made many a peanut butter and jelly sandwich for me in there. Both tugs had two-burner kerosene stoves to cook on.

While talking about food, I will skip ahead in time to when I worked on deck on the *Mariner* in the late thirties. When a tow job would take us out of town and meals had to be served, I was elected to do the cooking. It wasn't a tough chore but it did get touchy at times.

More often than not, one meal would be either pork or lamb chops, cubed steak or hot dogs with beans. Other than the "dogs," it would be the usual, potatoes—boiled or home fries—and maybe some string beans or canned corn. Coffee, bread, or buns would be for desert. It really was no big deal; things had to be simple, but nourishing. When things were ready, I would give a yell to Father down in the engine room and go up and take the

Tug *Mariner. J.L. Sutherland.*

wheel while Loren and he ate. When they were through, I would have what was left and then clean up the dishes. This got to be a real drag because I was left with little to eat; those two had a stroke on them like barnyard porkers. The next trip up the coast, we had to eat aboard and I fried up six chops and a 14-inch frying pan heaped with onions, of course with the usual odds and ends, including coffee and coffee rolls. As usual, Loren and my father ate first, and when the time came for me to sup, all there was left was maybe a little more than a tablespoon of onions, one chop out of six, and a small part of a potato.

Now, I thought it about time to change the way of doing the cooking and eating. The next time we had to eat aboard, I purchased six lamb chops. I cooked up the usual side dishes. When it was time to eat, I ate first and had my two chops and never said a word. I put my dirty dishes in plain sight. After they ate, Father made mention that this was a bit unusual, but he sure got the message. Things were divided up in a more equitable manner after that.

My brother Gene never was enthused about going on the tug. I have no recollection whatsoever of seeing him on the boat. Allen related to me a happening one time when they both were aboard, and of course more or less unsupervised. Allen somehow fell overboard between the tug and a vessel and immediately both were screaming their heads off. Dad came running, and in one fell swoop, took Allen either by the collar or by the hair of his head, and unceremoniously yanked him on board. To hear Allen tell it, Gene just froze and screamed. I suppose Dad chewed them out, but it was and is one of the hazards of boating.

Allen was very enterprising, and during the summer vacations, he had a cart with a copper wash boiler, which he filled with ice and tonic. Either Thomas Wilson or Blatchford's would supply him the goods, and he would peddle from the steamboat wharf to Parkhurst's railway. Ice carts were always around and cold drinks went like wildfire. He would start at Stanton's machine shop at the end of Bruce Place (which at that time was an extension of the old Wharf Street) and work his way along from wharf to wharf to the bottom of Duncan Street. He made a few bucks on the good days, and more than a few on real hot ones. In those days, a nickel or two on a bottle added up. He stored all his tonics in the lower floor of Sherm Ruth's building, which, incidentally, was part of the original Boston & Gloucester Steamship Co. shed, part of which burned on December 18, 1926. Pilferage was kept to a minimum; it was kind of an honor system.

A while ago I mentioned Stanton's machine shop, a small but efficient marine repair facility. It was owned and operated by Al Stanton, and had a couple of workers to make repairs on engines and other things. He was a very nice person. I used to go in his shop and watch the men working at the machinery. The tugs had a couple of spare cast-iron propellers stored there, leaning up against a telephone pole.

There was a two-story building to the right, and farther back, there was an open space. It abutted the A.W. Dodd & Co. fish glue manufacturers. Stored in that building was what

William J. Sutherland (on the right) pictured in front of the B & G Steamship Company freight sheds in 1926. *J.L. Sutherland.*

was left of crockery ware and other materials from the S.S. Hartwell gift shop. Seymour S. Hartwell had a dry goods and general housewares store. It was originally located, in 1902, on Pleasant Street, next to the post office. He later moved his business to his home at 9 Chestnut Street, just up from Chick's Roast Beef on Main Street. After he went out of business, Hartwell used this building for storage and it was in an abandoned state for many years. Investigation of the premises revealed dishes and display cases of all kinds. Needless to say, some people helped themselves to this treasure. I think I have some old Willowware dishes and one oak display case that is still in my cellar. There was an artist, I think named Ray Carter, who had a room and studio upstairs in the same building.

There were several old pilothouses on the vacant property adjacent to Sherm Ruth's building, Most of them came from vessels that went swordfishing and, for one reason or another, were left there to rot or were simply abandoned. Two of the better ones were joined together and for years this was the "home" of one Tom Benham. In the 1903 directory, there is a Thomas Benham, master mariner, boarded at 82 Duncan Street; this may well be the same gentleman. He was, in all respects, a character. The time I knew of him, he was sort of a watchman for the vessels around there. He had a stove and everything he needed to survive, but in the winters, it must have been hell. This shack had no insulation and had cracks everywhere that you could sling a cat through. My, but he was a tough old dog.

Father told me of one time that Tom was taking care of the dories in the dock alongside of where he was living. I suspect at the time, he must have had a few snorts more than enough. He passed out and ended up in the bottom of one of the dories, which had some fresh water in it. Now all this happened in the middle of winter. He sported a full set of whiskers and, while prone and somewhat helpless, the beard froze solid in the ice where he lay. When he came to, his yelling brought help, and someone chopped him out, none the worse for wear.

Moored on the east side of Sherm B. Ruth's property was the vessel *Claudia*. John Bishop in Vincent Cove built this pretty vessel, with a "clipper bow," for Sylvanus Smith in 1902. Not a vessel of great note, she did what she was designed for—fishing. Word was that she was sold sometime around 1917 or 1918 to New Bedford interests. For a time, she was in the Cape Verde packet trade.

For some years, the *Claudia* assumed "derelict status," and ended up grounded out far up in the slip near her place of "birth" in what was left of Vincent Cove. The WPA workers finally cut the vessel to pieces. Its remains lie somewhere under Rogers Street, just across from Dunkin' Donuts, and, ironically, but a few feet from where the keel was laid in the then-John Bishop yard.

When my brothers and I were kids, the *Claudia* was afloat and tied up at Ruth's. The rigging was cut away at the deadeyes, and during summer vacation, we would swing across the deck and drop into the water. It was great fun. I don't suppose her design was much different than most vessels in her day, but as I mentioned, she had a rather nice clipper bow. This vessel had no auxiliary power, and the expense to refit was prohibitive. That, and of course her age of 24 years, more than anything else, sealed her fate.

Tug *Mariner. J.L. Sutherland.*

Towing of fishing vessels in the harbor was tapering off with the introduction of diesel power. It was getting so that some owners in the fleet would pull their boats from wharf to wharf just to save $8. The only time some owners would call for the tug was in rainy or windy weather, and a number of them would forget that money was owed to the towboat company.

As the engineer on the *Mariner*, I well remember Father responding to a call down to the "Fort"—these were the piers down on Commercial Street. Easing up alongside of the vessel in need, he would get cash in hand before a line was made fast. Just imagine, if you will, in 1946, eight bucks for a tow anywhere in the harbor. With a smile on my face, I would lean out the engine room door and listen to all the excuses that were given. It didn't take long for Father to ring up a couple of bells, and haul out of there if they didn't pay up. He had the damnedest memory. If that same vessel wanted a tow two, three, even six months later, he would up the fee to make up for the time spent in the original call for a tow, in cash. No true Scotsman would let someone else get the upper hand.

Father and I have seen fishing vessels pulled from wharf to wharf, from the "Fort" to the railways, but only in good weather. Some of those vessel owners were some cheap. It was partly because of this that the towboat went out of business, that and the availability of fuel oil and the lack of coal barges.

Captain Simon Theriault, the gravelly-voiced owner-skipper of the *Joffre*, often stated that the smallest bill he ever had to pay was the towboat charges. His vessel had an engine that needed air to start it, and when he called, we came. He always paid cash.

The winters of the thirties around here were cold. It was normal to see the temperature go below zero days on end. Ice in the harbor would get to over a foot thick, and in some years, a few inches more. Vessels would be frozen in at their docks, and the tug was hired to break them out so they could go fishing. Coal barges and lumber schooners had to dock at the Gloucester Coal Co. and Griffins in Harbor Cove. Channels had to be cleared for them as well as for other harbor traffic.

In the winter of 1935–1936, from December 29 to February 27, it was particularly cold. From February 7 to 27, every day except three, the *Eveleth* was hired by the city to clear ice. This meant breaking up what had setup over night. It was an advantage to have an easterly wind so the ice would drift out of the inner harbor; otherwise, it would pile up eight to ten feet high.

To protect the stem from ice damage, there was a heavy bronze piece, fashioned around the stem, above and below the water line. Over this, an iron plate was made to fit around the stem and hung by chains from the guardrails. It extended about six feet back on either side, and below the water line to the foot of the stem.

The normal practice was to peel the ice, not hit it head on, because the plum stem did not allow the bow to ride up on the ice and break it down. How the tug held together with this battering is a tribute to the builders.

The south channel to Slade's would be first. At that time, the Fish Pier was nonexistent, so the ice would have to be broken out between Five Pound Island and Smokey Point out the North Channel. If the wind was in the northeast, the ice would have a chance to exit the inner harbor and free the fishing fleet.

I can recall the ice line early on as far as Ten Pound Island. A few short years ago, it was seen beyond that. Historical records note that in the years 1856 and 1857, before Dog Bar Breakwater was built, the ice line stretched from Norman's Woe Rock to the lighthouse at Eastern Point. And we think we have hard winters!

After breaking up the ice in the slips, the tug would get as far into the slip as possible. Then by making fast to the pier, the crew would turn the engine over at a good clip. The wake would drive the floes out into the harbor. This would give the barges room to dock.

During the big freezes, clearing out Annisquam River was done just about every day. Most of the gill-netters used the shortcut when fishing the bay. Still, there were times when, even with breaking up the overnight ice, it would be fruitless to continue this practice. The netters would just have to go around the breakwater to get to their fishing grounds, which added a few more hours to their daily trips. When the netters reached their dock, the nets were usually frozen. For a fee of about $5, the tug would arrive, applying hot water and steam on the nets under a tarp.

The tug hauled the empty barges and three-masted lumber schooners from Griffins and Gloucester Coal. Hands on the barges were not always sober when it was time to leave the

This 1946 shot of Gloucester Harbor includes vessels at the "Fort" and fisheries. *J.L. Sutherland.*

dock. However, a line would be put aboard, and the vessel would be pulled out stern first and swing them out into the channel facing as near as possible to a heading out the harbor. The bargeman would then walk the towline up on the foot-wide rail, the length of the vessel, and make it fast on the forward bitt. Under a very short towline, it would then be a matter of dropping the barge on the so-called "pancake grounds," where he would drop the anchor at the captain's pleasure.

As in previous times, we had let the barges go shortly after we passed Shag Rock (sometimes, tongue in cheek, called Arnold's Rock) on the end of Ten Pound Island, and they were on their own. At the proper time, the captain would let go the hawser and kick the "stopper" of the anchor chain. Normally the anchor would pay out until the captain thought he had enough scope and drop the pawl again.

On one occasion, unnoticed, the "stopper" snapped back on the chain after letting out only a few fathoms; the weakest link parted, and away went the anchor, minus a few links of chain. The barge drifted along toward the shore at Eastern Point, the captain none the wiser.

Fortunately, while hauling back the towline, I noticed what had happened, and we raced back to get another line on the barge. We finally stopped his headway and it was none to soon, for when the barge swung around he was within spitting distance of Black Bess rocks. We towed him a safe distance to the middle of the anchorage ground where the captain dropped his other anchor. I often wondered how he explained the loss of the anchor to his bosses.

All during World War II, diesel fuel oil was rationed. In order to get oil, stamps had to be issued for any number of gallons. This presented a problem at times, but as fishing vessels had priorities in the effort to feed the troops, they had more than enough, and with a little swapping around, say for a free tow now and then, stamps could be had.

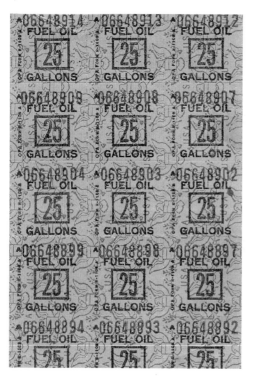

Typical fuel-rationing stamps used during World War II. *J.L. Sutherland*.

DOCKING THE BARGES

When the tug was hired to dock coal barges, it was always an interesting piece of work. Some, not all, of the barges were close to 300 feet in length and drew up to 16 feet or more when fully loaded. For a tug with only 160 horsepower, it took a world of experience to accomplish a docking without damage to barge or piers.

Most of the barges took on the lines of the old three-masted tern schooners, except that the bows were somewhat blunter but not with a plumb stem and, of course, no masts. The sterns, however, were of the pretty counter type and boasted huge rudders. The steering wheels were well over eight feet in diameter and were stepped down through a slot in the deck into a lower compartment so that the hub of the wheel would only be about four feet high. This is on the same idea as the configuration in the old steamboats on the inland rivers.

There were others, like the "Bee Line" scows. They were nothing more than square floating boxes. These barges were the only ones that were narrow enough to go through the railroad bridge in Manchester. The coal company was the Samuel George and Frank Knight Coal and Lumber Co., located at 36 Central Street.

On the day we were to dock a barge, the harbormaster would be notified, and he would start clearing out the channel. The tug would pick up the barge at Gloucester and head for Manchester. Anyone who knows Manchester harbor knows the yachts have a notorious habit of plugging up the channel. These "boxy" barges are hard enough to handle in airless weather, but in a 20-knot breeze, things can get out of hand.

A postcard showing Town Landing in Gloucester. *J.L. Sutherland*

As the barges themselves took the full width of the passage in the railroad opening, it was necessary to give the tow a slow push through the opening. The bargeman would then tie to the pier after clearing the draw. The tug would follow after and then lace up. If the harbormaster did his job, most of the anchored yachts were safely out of the way; if not, some paint was removed from the yacht hulls and the howls of the anguished owners could be heard for miles.

Within two to three days, when the time came to take the empty barge to sea, it was usual to lace up alongside and get to the bridge and moor it there while waiting for the next train to go by. When the draw was up, the tug would then move ahead of the barge and tow it astern to the "pancake ground" anchorage in Gloucester. The fee from Gloucester to Manchester and return was $85 each way. On occasion, the coastwise company tug would meet us at Newcomb's Ledge buoy, off Halfway Rock; that arrangement saved both tugs extra time.

Speaking of the coastwise tugs that dropped off and picked up the various barges, one of the prettiest of all tugs was the *D. T. Sheridan*. She was 109 feet long, with a 1,000-horse-power diesel engine. The *Sheridan* was single screw and had two stacks: one for the engine, the other contained the intake silencer. The *D. T. Sheridan* was built in 1939 in Brooklyn, New York, and was owned by the Sheridan Towboat Co. of New York. In November 1948, while towing a couple of coal barges in thick fog, she piled up on Monhegan Island. The coast guard failed in their attempts to free her, and it was a total loss. Fortunately, the barges were safely anchored.

I recall an incident when towing an empty barge out from Beverly. It was about abreast of Hospital Point, and the *D. T. Sheridan* had two other barges strung out astern of her, and was just idling along waiting for us. We were to bring our barge up to the trailing barge so a line could be passed and then we could cut loose and be on our way. This we did with no problem. We were running free and about abreast of Great Misery and Baker's Island, some three miles ahead, and here comes the *Sheridan*, "hooked up" towing three empty barges and edging right past us. She must have been doing 12 or 13 knots. As she passed, we gave our salutes; we were heading home to Gloucester, they, around the outside of Cape Cod to Norfolk, Virginia, for another load of coal. In about ten days or two weeks, the same barges would be right back.

A replacement tug, with the same name, was built in 1951—built in the same yard in Brooklyn, New York. She was 20 feet longer and had 1,600 horsepower. On the outside, she resembled her late sister, with the exception of only one stack.

Getting in and out of Beverly was relatively easy, though the channel was full of twists and turns. There were two separate coal companies in Beverly, the small one was named Girdler. Girdler, next to the bridge, usually had square "box" barges of the Blue Line, which featured what was called "Blue Coal." Almost every piece of coal had a fleck of blue dye on it. The name of the biggest coal company was Pickering Coal Co., the same as the one in Salem. Pickering had two unloading derricks. Girdler had only one. We were in and out of there at least once, sometimes twice a week.

There was a coal and oil company up the river in Danvers next to Route 114. We didn't do much work there. Ross tugs, *Betsy Ross* and *Eileen Ross*, did most of that docking, but at times there were occasions to go up beyond the auto and train bridges.

There were a few lumber schooners that serviced a dealer nearly in back of the Beverly depot. As soon as we cleared the bridges, it was a hard right and into the creek to the dock. This was always done at the top of the tide. What a mud hole!

Then there was Marblehead. The coal dock was way beyond the Eastern Yacht Club on the town side of the harbor. It is now the site of some condos. The anchorage in the harbor was just about everywhere, with no real channel to speak of.

The harbormaster was always a police officer, and I guess he tried to do the best under the circumstances. This is a town where the yachtsman ruled the harbor. There was always plenty of warning to move the anchored boats out of the way, but some took a hard line and didn't cooperate. Well, it was touch and go all the way. Many were the yachts that got rubbed on the way, both in and out. Funny thing, I don't recall a lawsuit that the company didn't beat.

Salem didn't have the yachts, but the coal dock was tucked away up near Derby Street. The wharf is still known as Pickering's Wharf. Derby Wharf was a granite-faced pier that began opposite the old customhouse and must be a couple of thousand feet long. A small lighthouse with a red light adorned the end. Docking had to be at high tide or the barge would take bottom. This would create a second attempt on the next tide, and a loss of revenue. The trick was to come in next to the corner of what is now Shetland Park, ring up full ahead and hard port rudder. As soon as that turn was made, it was full astern and a sharp right rudder up to the dock.

If it was done right, the barge would lie up nicely to the dock; if not, it hit the pier too hard and the coal tower would shake as if to topple over. When things didn't go as planned, there were a lot of anxious moments. Going out empty was much easier. The barge would be pivoted so the stern faced up toward the Congress Street bridge, then towed out by the bow to the anchorage in Beverly Harbor. The barge was usually the *Coaldale* from Penna.

The most unusual place to dock a barge was Lanesville—the so-called "hole in the wall." The tug would pick up the barge in Gloucester, and tow it around the cape. Close to the entrance, the tug would lace up on the port side and come straight on in. There wasn't enough room for tug and barge to pass through the gap, so just as the barge entered the gut, the tug would let go and tail after it on a snubbing line.

As the barge approached the coal wharf, the tug would stop the progress, and the barge hands would then warp vessel to the pier. All this was done at peak high tide. The barges would ground out in the mud at half tide. Going out light, it was a straight-out pull to deep water in the bay, and then the tow to Gloucester.

The barge usually was the *Tuckahoe*, and the charge, on May 11, 1937, for the tow from Gloucester around the cape to Lanesville, loaded, was $60. The return, seven days later, empty, was $55.

An early morning docking of a barge in Salem. *J.L. Sutherland.*

DELIVERING WATER

In the twenties, Ten Pound Island in the outer harbor had a coast guard air station and lighthouse plus a fish hatchery station. There was no water pipeline to the island, so all potable and boiler water to the fish hatchery and lighthouse had to be ferried out. The water was pumped into a cistern or tank under the house, and also to a water tank at the fisheries plant. Collected rainwater was never used.

The *Mariner* had a 3,300-gallon water tank that serviced the boiler when the tug had steam, and every so often, a load would be taken there. The towboat company would pay $1 for a thousand gallons, delivery would cost $15 for 3,000 gallons. In dry warm weather, deliveries would average out to about 15,000 gallons per month.

There were many trips to deliver water to the hotel on the Isle of Shoals. We would steam to Portsmouth and tie at the towboat wharf just above the bridge. We would take on 3,300 gallons of fresh water, and proceed to the hotel wharf. A round trip would take four hours: an hour to take on water, an hour to pump it into the cistern under the hotel, and two hours steaming out and in. I recall the four-hour delivery amounted to around $125.

If it were a particularly dry season, the need for water would warrant the services of the tug at least once, maybe twice. It was particularly dry in August 1941. We made five separate trips to Portsmouth, with multiple trips to the Shoals.

A postcard showing representations of the Boston & Gloucester Steamship Co. *J.L. Sutherland.*

Normally, all the buildings would drain rainwater from the roofs, and with filters, could, in a wet season, give them about all the water needed. Nature does not always cooperate. On the other hand, weather permitting, we were always available.

When we were delivering water, it was common to see the *Sightseer*, a pretty wood hull coal-burning passenger steamer, which carried visitors and freight from Portsmouth to the island. I believe that a religious group that summered there owned the steamer and three of the islands. A "new" *Sightseer* replaced that one. The last two were built of steel and were diesel powered.

The coast guard either owned or leased White Island and had a light and a house on it. Appledore Island was privately owned, as well as a small island owned by Ms. Celia Thaxter, the writer and poet. Duck Island was used as a bomb range for pilots out of Pease Air Base. There were a couple of other outcroppings and uninhabited islands that formed the group.

The fresh water was purchased at the Portsmouth towboat wharf just up river from the Route 1 lift bridge. When it was time to leave the dock, the tug would blow three blasts on the whistle, and in about ten minutes, the lift would open. This was standard procedure.

The current in the river was exceptionally swift and when the tide was ebbing, and in order to line up with the designated bridge channel, it was the accepted course of action to steam up river for some distance, make a fast turn, and then with fair tide and at normal engine power, make about 12 knots or better sailing through the draw.

There was and is now much marine traffic traversing the river. Two of the largest users are the Portsmouth Naval submarine base and an oil depot farther up the river. All large marine traffic up or down the river had to be made on high slack water.

One time, Captain Loren Jacobs cut the turn too soon, and before he knew it, the tug was broadside to the draw and hit the granite bridge abutment on the forward starboard quarter. Damage was severe. The crash took out ten feet of rail and stanchions, some decking, and cleaned the two guardrails and hull planking to the water's edge.

Fortunately, no seawater entered and the tug made its way back to the dock. A canvas patch was secured over the hole and it was sent home to Gloucester to make permanent repairs. I was not aboard when this incident occurred because I was in the service at the time. That incident took all the profit and more out of the contract.

I was aboard another time when we were filling water for the trip to the Shoals. Dad was to make a motor trip down east, and another engineer took his place. It was on the second day, and I had very little sleep. As deck hand, I was delegated to watch the filling of the tank and shut the water off when the tank was full. Provision was never made to have an overflow pipe installed over the side. I thought I'd rest a while and fell asleep.

It was fortunate that I woke up when I did; the tank was full and as there was no overboard bypass. The water then started to fill the hull. There was about a foot and a half of water in the bilge, floorboards were floating in good style. The deck was nearly awash, but no water entered the base of the engine, which saved a lot of cleanup time.

The engineer and I got the pump started and in about an hour and a half, cleared the water from the hull. Someone notified Dad at home, and on his way to New Brunswick, he stopped to see what had happened. Did I ever catch hell! After that, the chief and I took turns at the fill pipe.

At this period of time, most of our work was in Gloucester Harbor. Some of the vessels had engines that needed air to start them. The Fairbanks Morse engine on the towboat had a big piston air pump attached to the main engine as well as an auxiliary air pump. A hose would then be connected to the fishing vessel's air tanks, and gave them the needed air. The cost for air was the same as a tow, $8. If it took more than a half hour, the cost then tripled.

Vessels would also spring leaks, or sometimes a hose connection would let go or a valve would be accidentally left open and the ship would need to be pumped out. The company bought a two-inch portable pump, and this gave us good service. The *Naomi Bruce III* was near sinking one night at her berth in East Gloucester. Carl Peterson, the engineer, came aboard around four in the morning to go gill-netting. He found the engine room flooded and the deck nearly awash. He put in a frantic call for help. Father and I got the tug underway, and with the pump, we freed the boat of its water. A valve had accidentally been left open the afternoon before and the boat was open to the sea.

On another occasion, the 81-foot fishing vessel *Sebastiana C.*, built in Essex in 1932, was leaking badly and needed to be pumped out. Someone gave my name to the captain, saying that I had a pump, so he called the house. After the tug was sold, the portable pump was at home in the cellar. I was at home at the time and I had to get the pump and suction hose into the car and go to the Empire Fish wharf. When I arrived, and before I removed the pump from the car, I informed the owners of the charge: $25 for the first hour, $15 thereafter. That didn't go over too well, so I made a move to leave.

The insurance man arrived and gave the okay. I pumped, and in an hour and a half, the vessel was dry. They couldn't get on the railways because the tide was too low. I was ready to pack it in, but if the insurance man wanted me to stand by and pump once in a while, it would still cost $15 per hour or any part thereof. The vessel was finally hauled and the bill was for $85. It was paid in full, several weeks later. After I cashed the check, I notified the insurer that if any vessel insured by them was in trouble and needed to be pumped, it would be cash in hand payable every hour, on the hour, and portal to portal.

WORKING THE LINES

We had several deckhands over the years, but there were times when none were available. My father and I mostly did the towing around the harbor. When it came time to make up to a vessel, he would take care of the bowline, I would make up the spring and stern lines. Sounds complicated but it really was simple; we both knew what to do.

Any time we had to tow a barge by the stern bitts, a deckhand was needed because the hawser had to be manhandled aboard. If we were towing a square barge or lighter, a 30-

A 1944 receipt from Mariner's Towboat Company of Gloucester. *J.L. Sutherland.*

				MANAGER 76	OFFICE TELEPHONE 1320

Gloucester, Mass., April 25, 1944.
New Eng. Tel & Tel Company.
Tel Or. No. C. W. 2410.
U. S. Army Or. No. 2451.
Repair Cable Or. No. 970
Between Marblehead and Manchester.

In account with **Mariners' Towboat Co.**

Office, Wharf of B. & G. Steamboat Co.
Make checks payabe to Mariners' Towboat Co.

Harbor and Sea Towing

—— WATER ——

Mar.	29	Towing Army Scow Wonson to Fish Pier.		
		Transporting two coils of rope to Army Scow.		$25.00
Apr.	5	One day Repair Cable No. 970		$200.00
"		Use of Dory.		5.00
"	10	One day Repair Cable No. 970		200.00
		Use of Dory.		5.00
"	14	One day Repair Cable No. 970		200.00
		Use of Dory.		5.00
"	15	One day Repair Cable No. 970		200.00
		Use of Dory.		5.00
"	18	U. S. Army Scow Glo. to Boston.		-200.00
				$1045.00
		Certification on reverse side of bill.		

foot wire bridle was used. When the tow was completed, the bargeman let go the wires, which promptly sank.

Try hauling hand over hand about 250 feet or more of 6-inch hawser with wire on the end. It wasn't so bad in the summer, but in the winter, a frozen hawser is something else. It wouldn't coil; it would just go up both sides of the deckhouse and finally bend in a frozen heap. I would stand on the fantail, and call for a reverse of the engine. This would help by bringing the hawser to me. I had to be careful not to let the line go under the stern and foul up the wheel.

Several deckhands, Frank Pacheco, Walter Johnson, Louis Silva, Pete Lawson, and Al Menicocci were called on to do the chores. We also picked up a stray retired fisherman to handle the lines, but because they didn't have any idea what to do, it never worked out. Louis Silva was the finest one to work the lines.

SALT, COAL, AND LUMBER

There were also salt steamers to dock at Gorton Pews. It was kind of touchy once in a while. We didn't have a whole lot of power so we used the ship's propulsion ability to help out. I cannot remember any damage caused by any steamer to a dock while under the tug's care. When docking sailing ships, barks, and multi-masted schooners, it would get a little tricky. The towering masts and yardarms were great for catching any little breeze. Control was of the utmost importance, and at times, a tug from Boston would assist.

Coming in, it was a fairly straight approach to the dock. Going out, however, was somewhat different. It was a stern pull to what was called the deep hole in the middle of the inner harbor. After that maneuver, the ship was headed out and on its way.

In the twenties, it was nothing to have a half dozen or more salt steamers or barks come to Gorton's every year. In the late 1800s and up to the middle teens, it was the square-riggers and small steamers that brought the salt. In those years, there could be two or three barks at anchor in the outer harbor at a time. Most of the coarse salt came from Trapani, Sicily, and it was used primarily on the salting of cod. Some of the best salt did come from the north of England and was finely ground, just what was needed for salting mackerel.

Of course, not all of the sailing ships that visited this port were salt carriers. There were "coasters" by the dozen that were in the coal and lumber trade. In 1902, there were four major coal companies on the waterfront, and all had their deliveries by ship. Some of the "fore & after's" were so deeply burdened that they lay at anchor in either the inner or outer harbor while some of their cargos were off-loaded onto lighters before docking.

In 1902, one of the coal firms was the Frank Bennett Coal Co., at 43 Duncan Street. This firm filed for bankruptcy, and in 1903 was taken over by a consortium headed by Charles T. Heberle (treasurer and general manager) and Charles E. Fisher (president). Captain Heberle sold his interest in the Gloucester Towboat Co. to finance his part in the business. In 1902, Fisher was also the treasurer of the Gloucester Safe Deposit and Trust Co., a position that may have been some help in purchasing the business.

**RECEIVER'S SALE IN EQUITY
AT PUBLIC AUCTION**

In the Superior Court for Essex County. In the matter of Hazel A. Jacobs, Admx. vs. Mariners' Towboat Company. Equity No. 7827

**TOWBOAT
"MARINER"**

to be sold at

RUTH'S WHARF, GLOUCESTER, MASS.

SATURDAY, June 19, 1948 at 3 P. M.

The "MARINER" is a documented vessel, hailing from Gloucester. She is 64 ft. overall, 56 ft. 4 in. between perpendiculars and 15 ft. 3 in. beam. Her moulded depth is 7 ft. 6 in. and she draws 7 ft. aft. Her tonnage is 36.65 gross, 24 net. She was built at Essex by Arthur James, rebuilt in 1939 when she was converted from steam to diesel. Her stanchions, shear plank and topside have been rebuilt since then.

Planking is oak, 2½ in., frames 6x5 double-sawn on 21 in. centers. The deck is heavy, well-fastened to substantial deck beams and the planking is 3x2½.

She has a two cycle Fairbanks-Morse engine 160 h. p. new in 1935. Her fuel tanks are adequate, being two welded wing tanks in the shaft alley, carrying a total of 1,000 gallons. Her steel water tank forward has 3,000 gallon capacity.

The MARINER steers by hand gear, and is equipped with quadrant, rope, rods and chains. There is an oil-fired hot water heater which supplies heat to the pilot house via radiator. She has crew capacity for four men and a captain. There is an auxiliary bilge pump 3 h. p. which does duty as a washing down and fire pump and an auxiliary generator of 1½ k. w. She has also a 36 volt generator driven off the fly-wheel; also a set of Willard heavy duty batteries.

This vessel can serve as a waterboat, inland and outside tow boat, is handy, well powered.

Terms: Cash. Sale subject to confirmation by Essex Superior Court.

George F. Mahoney, Esq., Receiver
20 Pemberton Sq., Boston, Mass.

T. R. GROSSMAN & CO.—AUCTIONEERS
27 School St., Boston, Mass. LAfayette 3-5838

Notice of the sale of the tug *Mariner* from June 19, 1948.

J.L. Sutherland.

The firm was renamed the Gloucester Coal Co., and later, when the adjacent wharf was purchased for use as a lumber storage area, it was renamed again, this time to the Gloucester Coal & Lumber Co. Later still, the firm was renamed once again, this time the Building Center. The firm is still thriving to this day; the coal barges and lumber schooner trade is long gone, but it is still in the lumber and retail hardware business at the same location. All the lumber now comes over the road.

On June 18, 1947, the *Mariner* docked its last barge (the *Baltimore*, 2,215 tons) at this firm, and assisted it, empty, to anchorage three days later. On June 19, the *Mariner* delivered 3,000 gallons of water to the barge.

The Charles H. Boynton Coal Co. was located where the Benjamin Smith's playground is now situated. This berth was well up in Cripple Cove and could only be reached on the highest of tides. Still, the company flourished for a number of years. The Frank D. Griffin & Co. (known as Griffin & Company) was a major competitor in the coal business. It was located in Harbor Cove next to the town landing at 50 Commercial Street. A local businessman, Mac Bell is now the owner of the pier. Coal was their only business at that location, and the last recorded coal barge docked at that firm by the Mariners' Towboat Co. The *Mariner* docked the barge on September 8, 1942. It was designated as "Barge #9," owned by Lehigh & Wilkes Barre Coal Co. Its agent was the Cullen Transportation Co., 192 Lexington Avenue, New York City. The Griffin company was renamed the John

Alden & Griffin Coal & Oil Co.; Thomas Wonson was the president, and the business moved to Whittermore Street.

Charles Montgomery & Co. (at 12 Montgomery Place in East Gloucester) was another rival in the coal business. Oil, for the heating of homes, had not yet come into its own, and for some years these small companies faired pretty well. The town finally succumbed to the times and the coal companies failed. The Gloucester Yacht Yard now has its place of business in that location.

Sidney R. Harvey and Joseph E. Jones had a coal wharf in the so-called "hole in the wall" in Lanesville. In the 1902 directory, their coal and wood business was located at 804 Washington Street (at the rear), and after a time, it was taken over by another company and then disappeared completely.

The last entry for a coal barge to Lanesville was a Lehigh & Wilkes Barre barge, #7, towed from Gloucester to Lanesville on May 13, 1941. The fee for the tow was $60; $55 for the return trip to anchorage at Gloucester's "pancake ground."

THOSE AGING SCHOONERS

As the three- and four-masted coal and general cargo sailing schooners aged, the cost of upkeep to the hull and rigging became prohibitive. Soon, up and down the coast, vessels not fit for service were laid up at different locations. There were a couple in Boston Harbor, several in East Boston, and another one or two beached on the backside of Spectacle Island. Many of these old derelicts were anchored well out of the channels of Boston Harbor, and on one Fourth of July holiday, they were soaked with fuel oil and set on fire. It made a great show.

Two of the most famous coasters were the *Luther Little* and the *Hester*. Both, in the last stages of degeneration, lay in the mud of Wiscassett Harbor, Maine. A few years ago, the last vestiges of the vessels were set afire by vandals, putting an end to a tourist attraction never again to be duplicated.

One vessel of note that was tied to the north side of the old steamboat wharf for some time was the five-masted schooner *Cora F. Cressy*, built down in Maine in 1902. Her bow was as far up in the slip as she could go, and the stern hung out beyond the end of the pier by 50 to 60 feet. The coast guard ordered the watchman to hang a red lantern on the stern to warn the harbor traffic of the obstruction.

According to some old records, the *Cressy* was purchased by some Boston businessmen and was towed to Boston on January 26, 1929, by the tug *Nathaniel P. Doane*. Word was that the *Cressy* was transformed into the world's first and largest floating entertainment palace, and she operated successfully for several years off Point Pemberton and Nantasket. When last heard from in 1937, she was moored at some dock in Maine and was to be turned into a museum.

While the *Cressy* was moored at the old steamboat wharf, she was subject to the rigors of time and leaked quite a bit. Tugs used their steam siphons to free her of water. My dad told me about one time he was standing in the hold close to the keelson, a massive affair bolted to the full length of the keel, to give it added strength. He was over six feet tall and the keelson, and several sister keelsons, were well over his head.

This, and the keel itself, is the backbone of all wooden ships; it has to be very strong. Sooner or later, all wooden vessels, due to age or from grounding at berths, develop a noticeable "hump" in the vessel's shear line. This characteristic is called "hogging," it is bent in the middle so as to curve up like a hog's back. As far as I can recall, my father never gave me the impression that the *Cressy* suffered this condition.

When my brothers and I were young, Father and Mother took us on occasional jaunts to Essex to partake of the fried clams that made that town famous. Also, while passing through town and taking in the sights of the many vessels being built there, I well remember what I saw at the time. Here was a huge monster in the stocks and the bowsprit that hung well over the street. How were they ever going to get that boat out of Essex?

The launching and early career of the 164-foot *Adams* is well documented in the 1995 edition of *Shipbuilders of Essex*. She plied her trade until her return to Gloucester in 1932. She was then put up for sale. The sale price was finally set at $2,000, and the *Adams* went about her business until in December 1933, when she sank in the waters near Bermuda. In the records of the Mariners' Towboat Co., the entry reads "Schooner *Adams*, May 10, 1932—shifting anchorage in harbor." The fee was $6. The next entry: "May 16, stream to Gloucester Yacht Yard"; fee, $8. The next entry was on April 22, 1933—"Gloucester Yacht Yard to sea" fee, $12.

The *Adams* had been laid up at the East Gloucester yard for nearly a year awaiting a new owner, and as with vessels in long lay-up, the topside planking dried out. I remember us boys in a skiff going alongside of the vessel and pulling the long strips of oakum and cotton out of the seams. Before she could sail, most of the upper seams would have to be raked out and new caulking hammered in.

NORTH SHORE RELATIONSHIPS

The Gloucester Electric Company in early years had their electric generating plant and office at 22 Vincent Street, in the rear of where the Main Street office of Gorton's is now located. Later on, the offices of the Gloucester Electric and the Gloucester Gas Light Companies were located at 90–98 Main Street. The electric company abandoned the steam-generating plant and was renamed the Massachusetts Electric Co. Their main office is, I believe, in Malden. Vincent Street was the entranceway to the old Bishop's Ship Yard that was later filled in.

Father had told me that at the time a new company was formed, the Massachusetts Electric Co., the old steam-generating plant was unprofitable and was offered to the city for a song. The city fathers, in their infinite wisdom, turned down the offer as being too costly to run. Ipswich and other towns operated their own plants and did it with a profit, but our aldermen must have been on the conservative side.

Brookline with the Boston tug *Confidence* on December 18, 1930. *Dana Story.*

The electric company had its own pier, and coal was barged in and stored in a shed. The pier went into disrepair and finally disappeared with urban renewal.

Only one towboat, the *Mariner*, was in general use around the harbor. When the fish pier was in the process of construction, a cofferdam was built to set the perimeters of the area to be filled. A mud-sucker was used to not only fill the void, but to dredge the harbor at the same time. The tug moved the dredge from place to place as the need arose.

Harbor muck and water was pumped into the area described, and the accompanying water was allowed to escape through a sluiceway on the east side of the pier. Dredging was also done in the main channel, loaded into scows, and dumped at sea.

The last dredge that the tug *Mariner* serviced was a Randles & Co. clamshell digger. The dredging took place from April 22 until May 25, 1946. For the most part, it deepened Harbor Cove and there were two, sometimes three scows a day out to the disposal area about five miles southeast of the breakwater.

The first mention in the towboat company's record books of the towing of Gorton Pew's gurry scow by the *Mariner* was on July 7, 1944. During the summer months, June to October, when mackerel was being landed in great numbers, filleting went on and the waste was trucked off to some unknown dumping ground or in the harbor. Every fish concern was somewhat guilty of the practice and the harbor showed it. This is not to say that the industry was the only polluter. Before the main sewer lines were in use, there were many point sources along the shores of the harbor. It was a straight pipe system, and many

Two typical post cards of the era. The card above shows Annisquam Light in Gloucester; below is a scene of drying fish.

individual homes were piped into a "common" sewer. We have come a long way since those days. To Gorton's credit, it was decided that the best way to handle the situation was to buy a small, used three-bay mud scow. From May to early November of every year, until November 4, 1946, this process went on.

Depending on the amount of fish, the scow trips averaged two to three a week. At first the tows took about 2½ hours, emptying the scow about a mile or less outside the breakwater.

A muffled howl went up from the local lobster men, saying that the huge unending piles of gurry (or fish offal) on the bottom was feeding the lobsters and none were hungry enough to enter their traps for food. In order to quell the protest, the scows were taken out somewhat farther, which seemed to satisfy the grieved parties. When, in the off-season, the scow was idle, it was moored at the Slade Gorton pier in East Gloucester.

Gorton's had two "liver and spawn" collecting boats. Early on, one was operated by Joseph Paynotta, and another by "Paddy" Carr. Livers and spawns were saved by the gill-netters, sometimes as much as two to three barrels a day. The spawns were sold as a delicacy. The livers were processed into cod liver oil in a plant owned by Gorton's on Parker Street. The manager of the works was the late "Bob" Porper, the son of Captain Robert Porper.

A need arose to service these vessels, because most all of them, since the twenties, were diesel powered. There were at one time at least three fuel oil boats. Two of the important ones were the *Mayflower*, a wooden double-ender, which is long gone, and its replacement, the *Captain Dave*, which is still in business. The owner was David Lopes Maranhas. I'm not sure if the family still owns the business.

The *Captain Dave* was built in Ipswich in the Robinson yard, and was of steel construction. The boat is powered with a diesel engine, and must have come directly from the yards under its own power. Another oil boat was owned by William Nangle and berthed at Mellows Wharf, later the Empire Fish Co.

WORKING THE ESSEX RIVER

For a long time, coal barges and lumber schooners along the North Shore helped pay the bills. Essex and Ipswich launchings were later a mainstay of the towing business. The hazard of low water on the Essex bar and taking bottom was always a possibility.

To assist vessels entering the Essex River, a pilot had to be hired to see that the safest channel was marked out and to accompany the tug in and out again. The pilot that I knew was a fellow by the name of Thales Cook. I believe he held the title of harbormaster, probably because no one else wanted it. By profession he was a clam digger and was familiar with the bends and turns of the river. A few days before we were to tow a newly launched vessel out of Essex, he would mark the channel with tree branches at all the important turns of the river. We trusted that he was sober when he plied his channel-marking chore, because when he was on the tug, going in and coming out, he didn't have a leg under him. Marking the "upper" channel was of little concern to the coast guard, for they had only to buoy Essex River up to the Comono Point Gut.

The launching of the *Governor Saltonstall* in Essex on April 20, 1940. *R. H. McNeil*

The *Mariner* towing *Governor Saltonstall* in Essex on April 20, 1940. *R.H. McNeill.*

Opposite and Left: The schooner *Redskin* (previously *Governor Saltonstall*) near Black Bess outcroppings, *c.* 1946. *J.L. Sutherland*.

In the summer months, there were always a few selected guests that boarded the tug in Gloucester for the summer excursion to Essex. More often than not, the guests were friends of the Jacobs family, and always there was at least six or seven in number. The trip, if one could call it that, was often a sightseeing one. Going past Comono Point always was a greeting place; the folks on the shore waved, and the tug responded with a whistle or two. The tug would always try to get there a good hour or so before the launch, and if tied to a pier, some of our crowd would go ashore for a few minutes.

It was, more often than not, a stirring sight when the vessel slid down the ways. Those who have never witnessed a launching will most likely, with few exceptions, never have the opportunity to see one. Underway with the new vessel, past the Essex causeway, and again at Comono Point, the automobile horns and the tug's whistle gave a resounding salute.

Once safely over the Essex River bar, and if the tide permitted, it was through the Annisquam River under a short towline. On the other hand, if the tow got a late start and the vessel was of deep draft, it was an added two hours to the arrival time to go around "The Cape."

In the summer months, there was always a sea breeze in the afternoon and evening, and when rounding Thatcher's Island, it got a little sloppy, much to the chagrin of the "landlubbers." From Thatcher's to the Dog Bar Breakwater was less than an hour, so it was really no big deal. A couple of times when coming through the Annisquam River, the vessels would take bottom, but not enough to stop the tow.

Going through the B&M Railroad bridge was an art in itself. Shorten the hawser to about 60 feet or so, slow the tow to barely steerage way, make the widest turn to enter the gut, then full power. This maneuver allowed the vessel astern, with the help of its rudder, to tail along behind the tug and not veer to either side and hit the sides of the bridge fenders. It did not always work the way it was intended. With a fair tide, that is, tide ebbing and the current with us, it was hard to keep the tow in line.

One time a vessel rubbed the bridge fender on the port side, and the guardrail on the vessel rode up on the fender strip until the weight of the hull took effect and ripped the guard off the vessel, losing about 10 to 12 feet of it. Needless to say the price of the repair was borne by the company and as only $80 or $90 was the charge for the delivery to Gloucester, about all the profit and more was eaten up—most distressing!

However, most times, the job was uneventful, though there were occasions when it could get "hairy." We were bringing the *Kingfisher*, which was built for Lawrence C. McEwen and launched in Essex in March 1947. After a successful trip through the river, the vessel was under a towline astern, making about 3 or 4 knots.

About abreast of Tarr & Wonson's paint factory, it was usual to let go the hawser, make a quick 180, and lace up alongside. All the helmsman on the *Kingfisher* had to do was steer straight into the channel. Instead, with more than a few beers under his belt, he wasn't paying attention and drifted to starboard directly toward West Wharf at Rocky Neck.

Captain Sutherland (my dad) saw trouble in the wind, rang up full ahead to catch up with the wayward child. Louis Silva was our deckhand at the time and had a line ready to pass to anyone handy. It was made fast on the cleat on the aft "gallows frame," and with full reverse stopped the vessel within inches of the pier. Had the vessel collided with the old and shaky wharf, the pier and apartments that adorned it would surely be in the drink.

When we were out of danger and the tow dead in the water, my father was out of the wheelhouse and trying to get up on the vessel to get at the man at the helm. Fortunately, for that guy's sake, the side of the vessel was too high for my father to scale, but after a series of raucous epithets, he calmed down and finished the tow. As soon as the vessel was secured to the wharf, the helmsman vanished.

It is interesting that in 1996, 49 years later, this same wharf, with its 20-odd apartments, made some startling news. The ravages of time, and some questionable repair work, finally worked its will, and the building and wharf, acting much like the launching of another vessel, slipped its moorings, and took the final plunge into the harbor, unassisted. It was considered most fortunate that no one was seriously injured.

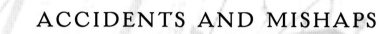

ACCIDENTS AND MISHAPS

6

Accidents are not unknown to the vessels of Gloucester. Some of them could well have been prevented. There is a well-worn adage, "Familiarity breeds contempt." This proved true in the incident that happened one day on the vessel *Jackie B.*, which was moored at the then-Sherman Ruth's Wharf. The vessel was at times a gill-netter, seiner, and lastly, a small dragger. The principal players were Sherman B. Ruth, the owner of the wharf; Jack Barrett, the owner of the vessel; and another person, probably the engineer.

The gist of the story is that they were testing engine nozzles to see if they were atomizing correctly before installing them in the cylinder heads. The process involved actuating the mechanisms, and in so doing, the engine room slowly was filled with a very fine mist of diesel oil. This mist was so fine that it went unnoticed in the darkened engine room. It also presented an explosive atmosphere, and one that could have been avoided if the testing was done on deck or in the adjacent machine shop.

The sequence of events can only be guessed at. It was not unusual that when starting a cold diesel engine, a coffee can with oily rags were hung on the air intake ports and set on fire. At the lighting of the rags, ignition was initiated, and a violent explosion and flash fire occurred. As there was really no time to exit the engine room so as to escape the consequences of their actions, Sherman Ruth died as a result of his burns. Barrett was also critically burned along with the other person.

Another instance I well remember was when working part time in the machine shop at Ruth's wharf. It involved the usual practice of hanging coffee cans with some small oily rags in them near the breather intakes of diesel engines. The vessel *R. Eugene Ashley* was a New Bedford-based vessel fishing out of Gloucester and powered by a really old Atlas. It was notoriously hard to start, especially in the winter. When the starting air pressure was pumped up, the oily rags were ignited on all six cylinders. The subsequent heat in the

The *Rosalie S.* was built by John F. James & Son for the Consolidated Lobster Co. and launched on March 16, 1925. It operated as a "wet well" lobster carrier between Maine and Bay View in Gloucester before going down. The author was engineer for two years when the vessel was owned by Joseph Parisi & Sebastian Scola. *Gloucester Daily Times*.

The tug *Mariner*, alongside *Jackie B.*, in 1945. *J.L. Sutherland*.

intake air usually gave enough impetus to start it up. This action created plenty of smoke to breathe, but offered little danger.

There is always some unrelated event that arises at the oddest times that has nothing to do with towboating, but it is a side issue that takes on the cloak of slapstick comedy. You really had to be there to appreciate it.

While I was working on the *Mariner*, our berth was on the east side of the Ruth wharf. The vessel *Evelyn G. Sears* was also berthed at Sherman B. Ruth's Wharf. A.D. Story built the vessel in Essex on November 21, 1925, for the Sears family of Gloucester. It was a small schooner type, only 71 feet in length, powered by a 140-horsepower Atlas diesel engine. This vessel was made famous in that on one of her many swordfishing trips, she stocked more than any other vessel in the business, and also held the record in number of fish caught on one trip.

To get to the meat of the story, there was a gentleman who lived in Essex who was the engineer on the *Sears*. The chief saved about two-dozen swords from one of the trips, with the intent to take them home, sell them later, and make a few bucks. First-rate straight swords could bring several dollars, those with a curve, much more.

As the swords were "green" they had to be "cured." This involved placing about a dozen swords in each of two burlap bags and hanging them under the wharf below the low watermark. This "curing" took about a month or more, allowing the "marrow" in the bones to set.

This did not go unnoticed by me, and it set the mind on a plan to relieve this chap of his goods. There were times when the tug would berth adjacent to where he hung the bags, and unobserved by my dad, I then slipped them aboard. There was some slight danger that it could point the finger at perhaps a single culprit: me. This point had to be addressed. Of course, between the time the *Sears* left on another trip and returned, other vessels would take her berth, and in so doing, expand the number of potential suspects.

When the *Sears* came to port and berthed at the usual place, the absence of the bags would be noticed immediately, and then all hell would break loose. This event would have to be delayed. I brought a half dozen red bricks from home, and after removing the swords, and swapping the contents with the bricks, put the bags back in the proper place to give the appearance that all was well.

A few weeks later, when the unsuspecting chief retrieved the bags, all hell did break loose. Needless to say there was plenty of finger pointing as to just who the culprit was, but fortunately, I escaped scrutiny. I have a couple of the swords yet, curved ones at that.

The chief acquired plenty more swords, enough in fact to make a picket fence out of them. He has departed from this world, as well as his fence, and I'm only telling this story now because the statue of limitations is no longer in effect.

Early in the century, Gloucester Harbor bustled with many tugs; some just to move a vessel from one wharf to another, others to tow beyond the harbor limits. Not a whole lot of money was made in many of the undertakings but it served a purpose as well as put food on many tables.

As the middle thirties approached, tow jobs were getting scarce. A contract to haul stone to Newburyport for the breakwater was most welcome. However, it did not come without its problems.

It started in Gloucester on May 4, 1937, when the Cape Ann Granite Co. secured the services of the tug *Mariner* to tow scows, loaded with grout, to repair the Newburyport breakwater and, of course, return. For the better part of five months, often less, but not spaced more than three days apart, this tedious chore went on without mishap, week after week.

The tug would pick up a flat-decked scow, about 115 feet in length, loaded with granite boulders called "grout." We left from the "hole in the wall" in the village of Lanesville, for a two- to three-hour trip; every tow much the same as the ones before and the ones to follow.

On this particular day, the *Mariner* left Lanesville at or about 7 a.m. on October 20, 1937, with a loaded scow, bound for Newburyport. The tug arrived at the bar and the tow was turned over to another tug, the *Beetle*. Some hours later the tug picked up another scow, no. 28, which was light, and proceeded back toward Lanesville. The scow was admittedly old and leaky, but not unseaworthy for the short nine-and-a-half-mile trip.

At the time, the *Mariner* was about 30 years old, originally built in 1909 as a steam tug. It had been fitted with a diesel engine of 160 horsepower about six months previous to this event. The weather was acceptable at the time of departure, and the prediction was for fresh to strong south to southwesterly winds, shifting to westerly late in the day. As with modern weather reports, some are not very reliable—some today are not much better than those in 1937.

The winds increased sooner than expected, and the seas became quite choppy. The scow, with its high freeboard acting like a sail, restricted the tug's forward progress. There was no place to go but straight ahead. The thought of turning back was out of the question, for the bar at Newburyport would be breaking and the tide was on the way out, adding to the normal rip tide.

Anyone familiar with two-cycle Fairbanks Morse engines knows they are prone to carbon up the stack, and when the engine is forced, the oily carbon ignites. This, in itself, in not troublesome, it just burns itself out in time. To ease the amount of fire in the stack, the engine is slowed to barely turning over, reducing the amount of oxygen feeding the combustion.

During the daylight hours, the normal amount of smoke emitted from the stack reminds one of an efficient coal-burning tug. At night, no smoke is seen, but the showers of sparks and flame when the stack is afire is akin to the Fourth of July fireworks, but assuredly, nothing to be really concerned about. Buckets of seawater were passed to me on the top deck, and the canvas deck cover and the lifeboat cover were wetted down. Small chunks of half burned carbon would have to be extinguished. But this was only part of the problem. The hours passed by, and darkness was slowly approaching.

At about 5 p.m., the coast guard cutter *Harriet Lane* was standing by at this time, having been alerted by someone ashore. I have a suspicion that the smoke and sparks from the stack caused someone to call the coast guard. About that time, men on the cutter noticed that the scow was settling deeper and nearly awash. It now was around 6:30, when the cutter lowered a boat and took aboard the two crew members, a man and his wife.

The scow, constructed of long-leaf pine, had at the time its customary ten feet of free-board; then within minutes, it was deck level with the sea, and it was thought a plank let go. The scow was set adrift and was beached on Wingaersheek Beach. A day or two later, the tug came back and I went on board to secure the towing hawser. In the small deck-house, I picked up an Enfield rifle. It was pretty well rusted up, and I gave it away a few years ago. The half sunk scow was then towed to Gloucester harbor where it lay awash at anchor off Five Pound Island for two years.

Finally, Bill LaFond acquired the scow to store his small boats on. He hired the tug *Mariner* to tow the scow up the river and deposit it on the marsh where the Cape Ann Marina is now. He wanted it to lie alongside of the granite sloop *Herbert*, which he bought for $1, and both are buried somewhere under the marina's office.

The court absolved the Mariners' Towboat Co. of any blame, for the scow was in terrible shape. Though thought to be seaworthy, the scow was an accident waiting to happen.

Due to the nature of the business, all tugboats lead checkered careers, and the Mariners' Towboat Co. tugs were no exception. It was some time in 1936, and the steam tug *Eveleth* was to tow a McKee lighter from Gloucester to Newburyport.

This lighter was similar to all A-frame, floating derricks. Exact measurements of the size of the hull are not at hand, but the hull was approximately some 45 feet in breadth and a good 125 feet in length, drawing perhaps 4 feet forward and 6 aft. In this case, this lighter had an exceptionally large house, leaving only enough on either side for a walkway to the after mooring bitts. The house was built around the A-frame and was conservatively 20 feet high, enough to clear the steam boiler and hoisting gear inside. Similar to a barge, it was built like a box.

The *Eveleth* was the typical steam tug of the day—63 feet in length and powered by a 160-horsepower steam plant. The tug coaled up at the Gloucester Coal Co., topped off on fresh water the day before, so as to get an early start. The day started out well. The crew was Captain Loren Jacobs, Mate Bill Jacobs, and Engineer William Sutherland, my brother Roy as the fireman, and myself for the ride. The weather forecast was favorable: wind southerly 10 to 15 knots, shifting to the northwest 25 to 30 knots late in the afternoon.

The breadth of the lighter prohibited the transit of the Annisquam River, so around the cape it was. We picked up our tow around five in the morning, and proceeded out the harbor. The progress to Thatcher's Island was uneventful, and Jake had said later that we were making about 6 knots, wind on the quarter, not at all bad for the size of the tow. As the tow neared Thatcher's about ten, the western sky took on an ominous look, and it wasn't long before things happened.

Wind and sea picked up. Still it didn't look like we couldn't make our way. We had slowed ever so slightly going past the salvages, a small island and of a group of shoals to the northwest of Thatcher's Island. The tug was now entering Ipswich Bay and it received the full brunt of the northwest wind. The tug's engine was then at full ahead. Perhaps the

A newspaper photograph showing the tug *Eveleth* in Gloucester Harbor. *Gloucester Daily Times* *(Ben Goldman Collection)*.

front would pass and things would quiet down. The tow would be a little late, but that's the nature of the business.

Our progress was slowed to a standstill, and it wasn't long before we started ever so slowly to drift backwards. The house on the lighter was acting like a big sail, and with the increasing winds, the inevitable happened. If this kept up, we may have ended up on Cape Cod.

The *Eveleth* was built as a harbor tug, with the after towing bitt's well toward the stern, good for lacing up to a vessel, and doing its job as intended. Outside modern towing tugs have their towing winch or after bitts well up in the middle of the hull. This arrangement allows the tug to pivot easily, and change directions at will.

For the *Eveleth* to make a turn in a windy situation, it had to back down and try to get in the desired direction. In this case, this was impossible. The only other options were to either cut the hawser and come alongside of the lighter and try to get back to the west side of Thatcher's, in the lee of the land, or signal for help. The latter was chosen and having no ship-to-shore radio, it was the upside-down American flag on the staff. We hoped someone would see it.

Fortunately, the keeper on Thatcher's Island was alert, and it became known later that he was following our progress for some hours. He called Base Seven in Gloucester, and a "Six-Bitter" (75-footer) was sent out. When he came alongside, against Captain Jacobs's wishes, he put a tine on our forward bitts, laid out a length of line, and started to pull. These 75-foot coast guard patrol boats were powered with twin Sterling gas engines, and if he went straight ahead, that was fine. However, he veered somewhat to port trying to turn us toward the west, and in doing so levered the *Eveleth* over on her port beam to a precarious angle. When Jake saw what was happening, and the port deck was awash, he yelled to Bill Jacobs, the mate, to get the fire ax and cut the line. This was done, and the tug righted itself. All the time this was going on, we were still going backwards, and no nearer a solution to the problem.

The coast guard picket boat came alongside, and Jake chewed the skipper out something fearful. He said if he wanted to help, to go to the starboard side of the lighter and get a line on her forward bitt and pull. This would give the necessary pulling power and tend to turn the lighter to the west, the only possible way to get into the lee of the cape, and head for home.

It was 10:30 that night when the tug secured in Gloucester, after 17 hours of hard pulling and no farther ahead. The bunkers were nearly empty, maybe a half a ton or less of coal left. My brother Roy, the fireman, was dogged out. My dad did give him a shift or two, but for the most part, he shoveled about eight tons of soft coals into that furnace.

Two days later, when the wind died, the trip was started again. This time, all went well. Needless to say, the costs relating to that first struggle were swallowed by the company.

THE M.S. *RIO BRANCO*

Early in the morning of September 17, 1939, the Norwegian-registered diesel motor ship *Rio Branco*, of some 3,200 tons, on a trip from Para, Brazil, to Boston, apparently in a clear starlit night, fetched up on the back shore of Cape Ann, in front of Arthur Leonard's estate, just northeast of Eastern Point light. There are variations as to how the incident happened, but it was generally agreed that Captain Thor Orvig mistook Eastern Point light for Grave's Light, at the entrance to Boston Harbor.

Some residents heard the grinding of the iron hull against granite as the ship came to a halt. Others thought they heard identical noises at two separate, but closely related times. Accounting for two separate grindings, this would mean that the ship perhaps was relieved of her stranding, and not having acquired enough sea room, fetched up again. There was no evidence that this in fact happened. What was viewed at daylight was a freighter of some 3,200 tons in Mr. Leonard's front yard, so to speak.

The vessel was holed in the three forward compartments, and to refloat the vessel, it was agreed that some of the stores had to be off-loaded. Jettison of some of the cargo without fanfare—getting the ship afloat was the primary concern.

A call went out to the coast guard, and finding that the vessel was in no immediate danger, the towboat *Mariner* was called to assist. There was nothing this small tug could do to pull a ship of that size off of the rocks, so another call went to the Boston Towboat Co. In a few hours, the relatively new Boston Towboat Company's diesel electric tugs *Venus* and *Luna* were on their way. Merritt, Chapman & Scott had two tugs and two lighters already on the way. The larger of the two tugs was a former navy steam salvage tug named the *Peacock*.

M.S. *Rio Branco* on September 17, 1939. *Steamship Historical Society of America Collection.*

Author's photograph of the M.S. *Rio Branco. J.L. Sutherland.*

The Boston tugs were "sister" tugs, and both hulls were painted white with varnished upperworks and red trim, including black stacks. They were a pretty picture. Each was powered by twin eight-cylinder Winton diesels driving two G.E. generators, which in turn supplied electricity to a mammoth motor directly connected to the propeller shaft. At the time, they were the most powerful of the Boston Towboat Co. fleet. While they were stationed in Gloucester, I had the pleasure of viewing these two tugs from top to bottom. At the time, they were indeed the ultimate in towing vessels. I noticed not long ago in the news that the hulks of both tugs were in the shallows of the Charles River, somewhere above the locks. The *Luna* was raised and sent to Maine to be rebuilt. It is now back in Boston and in great shape.

Meanwhile, the *Mariner*, owing to her shallow draft, acted as messenger to bring representatives of the ship to and from shore. It also assisted insurance agents in the same capacity. Early on, the services of Merritt, Chapman & Scott were acquired. Before their vessels arrived, salvage experts were rushed to Gloucester and ferried to the ship by the tug *Mariner*.

When, after a few days, it became apparent that indeed some of the cargo had to be lightered off, the *Mariner* assisted the lighter *Philip* to the forward port side, to take whatever the salvagers offered.

A close-up of the M.S. *Rio Branco* from her starboard side.
J.L. Sutherland.

The *Mariner* also assisted the huge Merritt, Chapman & Scott salvage lighter to the starboard side of the ship. As the ship was hard aground on good Cape Ann granite, and in no danger of sinking, its own cargo booms shifted some of the cargo to a better location, so as to reveal the extent of the damage to the hull.

Quite a lot of castor beans, mixed with cocoa beans, was discharged over the side, either by accident or design, and were floating in a brown mass along the shore. Some may have escaped through the gaping holes under water. The gulls were having their fill, and the results in the next several days were many dead birds littering the shore. Of course, there was no way to stop this, so it ran its course. It was mentioned around that some of the locals tried some of these "goodies," and to their dismay, found that castor beans caused a great deal of discomfort.

The freighter was carrying a general cargo. Besides the approximately 225 tons of wheat bran, castor and cocoa beans, there was any number of hides and raw latex rubber balls. Also on board were 5 passengers and a crew of 29 Norwegians, besides the captain, mates, and engineers.

The crude rubber balls were for the most part kept on board the ship, some in different compartments below decks. As the salvagers moved them from one hold to another, a

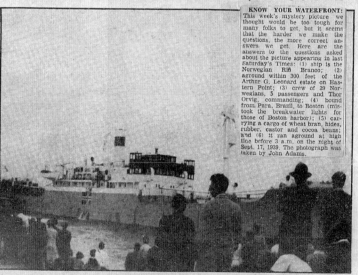

These beans never made Boston

By BETH ALBERT

The beans were spilled in Gloucester harbor 40 years ago. That is, castor oil beans.

At least Paul Kenyon of 6 Nashua Ave. believes that is what lighted from the SS Rio Branco after the 3,200 ton Norwegian freighter went aground near Eastern Point in 1939.

Remember when

Joseph Garland disagrees. In his book, "Eastern Point," Garland states that 225 tons of cocoa and bran flooded the harbor.

Janice Nugent of 194 Eastern Ave. was just 11 years old when the freighter landed on a ledge about 300 feet in front of Arthur Leonard's Druimteac. She doesn't know if the beans were coffee, cocoa or castor oil, but she does remember that no one was supposed to eat them.

Ms. Nugent went with her mother to Eastern Point to watch the Coast Guard struggle to put the freighter afloat. She was part of a crowd of thousands that watched the Coast Guard work for a week before the boat moved. The crowds caused such a traffic jam that the police banned cars from the Point.

The Rio Branco, steaming from Para, Brazil for Boston, kept close to the coast to avoid German U Boats. The morning of Sept. 17, Captain Thor Orvig kept the boat a little too close.

KNOW YOUR WATERFRONT: This week's mystery picture we thought would be too tough for many folks to get, but it seems that the harder we make the questions, the more correct answers we get. Here are the answers to the questions asked about the picture appearing in last Saturday's Times: (1) ship is the Norwegian Rio Branco; (2) aground within 300 feet of the Arthur G. Leonard estate on Eastern Point; (3) crew of 29 Norwegians, 5 passengers and Thor Orvig, commanding; (4) bound from Para, Brazil, to Boston (mistook the breakwater lights for those of Boston harbor); (5) carrying a cargo of wheat bran, hides, rubber, castor and cocoa beans; and (6) it ran aground at high tide before 3 a.m. on the night of Sept. 17, 1939. The photograph was taken by John Adams.

Around 3 a.m., according to Garland's book, the watch spotted a light. Thinking it was Boston Harbor, the helmsman headed for it. A few minutes later, the 29-member crew and Orvig heard the crunch and screech of steel.

The light watch had seen

Eastern Point; the freighter was 20 miles off course.

A swell from the Northeast ground the vessel against the ledge. The pumps couldn't keep up with the incoming sea. After three days of failure, the Coast Guard lighted the vessel of 3,000

bags and beans, according to Garland.

With her pumps disgorging streams of water, the Rio Branco steamed around Eastern Point, a week after she went aground. In three days, the freighter would be on her way to Boston.

The Rio Branco leaves Gloucester Harbor in 1939 after a three-day delay   Photo by Janice Nugent

Newspaper clipping showing the M.S. *Rio Branco* run aground on September 17, 1939. *Gloucester Daily Times.*

few of them did get overboard, and my father, my brother Roy, and I picked one up. The rubber would barely float, and in order to get one aboard, a pipe was slipped through the center, and with ropes on the ends of the pipes, it rolled up and over the tug's rail.

These balls of crude latex must have weighed well over 100 pounds, and the struggle was hardly worth it. I kept the rubber ball at home for a number of years, and I finally gave it away to someone from Eastern Point whose name escapes me.

One other thing I have to mention was that some small part of the cargo was cashew and pecan nuts, put up in five-pound tins about the size of one-gallon olive oil tins. The salvage crew was helping themselves to tins, and while alongside, they tossed several cans down to us on the tug. Now, when eating these rich, shelled nuts, we made sure to curb our yen for these goodies, and for a good many weeks, mother doled them out.

The towboat records of those days show that from September 17 to the 26, services were rendered by the tug *Mariner* to the *Rio Branco*. The two Boston tugs, *Venus* and *Luna*, were standing by in Gloucester Harbor to render any assistance needed.

When the time neared to free the ship from the shore, activity by attendant vessels increased. Two large "Dunn" kedge anchors were placed by the lighter *Philip* some distance astern with one-and-a-half-inch wire cables attached. These anchors also had "tell-tale" buoys and wires attached to them for retrieval purposes. The wire cables were secured to a winch on the stern of the *Rio Branco*, and would exert a strain when the time was at hand. The two Boston tugs trailed out long lengths of ten-inch manila hawser. (Nylon was not around then.) Some seven days passed, and the time had come to act. The winches took their maximum strain; the four-cylinder 6,000-horsepower Krupp diesel engine, deep in the bowels of the ship, came to life at full astern. The two tugs backed and with slack in their lines, tried to exert a surge jump and after several more pulls, plus the last of the incoming tide, the effort proved successful and the vessel cleared the ledges. With a number of pumps doing their job, the ship slowly inched its way off of the shore, and once again, though holed in several places, and leaking somewhat, she was again in her own element, afloat on the briny.

As I recall, the vessel was eased around the breakwater and either anchored close to, or grounded on Nile's Beach. For the next three days and nights, the temporary cement patches on the ruptured plates and welding of the torn bottom plates continued and was stiffened to a sufficient degree of seaworthiness for the trip to Boston and dry-docking.

While the ship was hard aground on the backshore, I was fortunate to be invited to view the engine room. It was immaculate. The cylinders were big enough to fit four good-sized men in at the same time. Two spare cylinder heads and two spare pistons were hung on the bulkhead, along with the wrenches that took a couple of men to handle; it was quite a scene. Little English was spoken, but the sight of the well-kept engine room was all one could ask for. Here was a four-cylinder marine engine two stories high, generating 6,000 horsepower. Our tug, also with a four-cylinder marine engine, generated only 160 horsepower.

The chief of the vessel was dressed in "whites," and the second and third engineers were dressed in blue coveralls and bow ties. I would say that discipline was strict aboard this ship.

As one can readily see, the *Mariner* had little to do with the actual salvaging of the ship. On October 26, the *Rio Branco* was off to Boston and in a dry dock.

As for the two kedge anchors, one is still out there, having jammed itself in the ledges. The one retrieved by the *Philip* was gently placed on the bow of the *Mariner*, and on November 6, 1939, was taken to Boston. The tug presented a rather odd sight, with its bow down to within two feet of its bow guard, and the stern up in the air far enough to cause a "rooster tail" wake. There was an abbreviated accounting of the event in the *Cape Ann Summer Sun*, dated August 31, 1979; but one actually had to be there to give a full account of the everyday activities.

THE *VENTURE II*

The fishing vessel *Venture II*, 99 feet, 118 gross tons, was launched at Damariscotta, Maine, in 1930. It was built for Lawrence W. Soule of Boston. This was a successful vessel, and went about her trade unnoticed—that is, until early in October of 1946.

In the Mariners' Towboat journals, there is no notation of towing or assistance rendered to this vessel throughout her years, although she was a yearly visitor to be refurbished at our local marine railways, mostly at Burnham's.

After the usual overhaul, she set sail for her port of Boston sometime in late September or early October, with a two-man crew, enough to make the trip. I don't recall the exact date of her "sinking," but reference can be made in the local paper of that time. It seems something was amiss in the engine room, and a call for help went out saying something to the effect that the vessel was taking on water. The vessel's position was a mile southwest of the bell buoy off of Norman's Woe, an island made famous by Longfellow. The vessel sank, with only the mastheads a few feet above the surface.

The first mention of the unfortunate event in the towboat records is on Monday, October 7: "Lighter *Jupiter*—4.5 hours," the tow from Boston. This was a heavy-lift steam lighter, owned by the McKee Co., and capable of salvaging this vessel if they could get the necessary straps under the hull. The moorings were set to position the lighter over the ill-fated vessel. For about nine or ten days, the crew of the lighter and divers labored to pass slings under the hull. It was nearly time to raise the *Venture II*.

Meanwhile, for a number of days, starting on October 9, the *Mariner* conveyed men and equipment, plus, 7,000 gallons of water (on different occasions) to feed the lighter's steam boiler. The days went by and on Saturday, October 19, the vessel was raised and secured to the side of the lighter. From the time of the initial hoist and the start of the slow three-mile tow to Niles Beach, it took 11 hours and 15 minutes—from 10:30 in the morning until 9:45 in the evening—when the *Venture II* was resting on the sandy bottom of the beach, her decks awash.

As the tide receded, leaving her deck free of seawater, pumps were put in action, and at the same time, divers went into the engine room to try and determine the cause of sinking.

As for the original two crewmen, they were nowhere to be seen. Much to the surprise of the insurance agents who were there, it was reported by the divers that for some mysterious reason, the several bolts securing the seacock were missing, which allowed the sea to pour in. New bolts were installed, and the vessel was pumped dry as a bone. It was argued that the machinists never secured the seacock at the start of the trip—a lame excuse, for if that were the case, the *Venture II* would have sunk at the dock.

She was taken to the marine railways for a general house cleaning. What happened to the two hands that were initially involved I can't say, but owing to the fact that no insurance was forthcoming, I dare say their fishing days were numbered. Work for the lighter was finished, and on Sunday, October 20, the *Mariner* towed *Jupiter* to Boston.

The record shows that on December 11, 12, and 19, 1946, the *Venture II* was towed to different piers to facilitate the overhaul efforts and make her seaworthy once again. That was the last time she made the news.

THE *ONWARD*

Occasionally the tugs did some long towing jobs. There were many to New Bedford; one I knew was to Bridgeport, Connecticut. There were also a few to places like Bar Harbor, Portland, Thomaston, Rockland, and Friendship, Maine, to pick up newly launched vessels for Gloucester.

One, I recall, was a short trip on October 14, 1941, to Cape Cod Canal. The job was to pick up a small tug and tow it to a place called "Butt's Yard" in Quincy. The 60-foot tug *Onward* had fetched up and sunk on the riprap of the canal. Some people in the Boston area purchased it for $750. She was raised and patched and needed to be pumped every four hours to free her of some three feet of water. After the agent of the owners assured Captain Jacobs that there were two pumps aboard to keep the tug free of water, the tow was started.

The tow was uneventful up the south shore with the wind astern until approaching Point Allerton, when the wind shifted more to the southwest and with it, a squall condition. The pumps happened to be on the port or windward side of the tug, and taking some spray over the rail, they were put out of action. Later, a witness testified that water was getting ahead of them before the loss of the pumps, and he suspected that the underwater "patch" had come off.

With the pumps out, sinking was a definite possibility. Acknowledging the plight of the crew, Captain Jacobs picked the two crewmen off and proceeded to tow the sinking tug toward "Nut" Island in Quincy Bay. This area afforded a muddy bottom, with few rocks to further damage the hull. When the captain got the tug as close to the beach as possible, Jacobs reversed the *Mariner*. After pulling as much of the hawser as possible aboard, Jake ordered me to cut the hawser. Within seconds, down she went, the two little masts sticking out of the water. The resulting lawsuit found the *Mariner* faultless, with costs. That's the last I ever heard of the *Onward*.

THE *POLLYANNA*

There were times when my father, the captain, and I, the engineer, of the *Mariner* had a few run-ins. One in particular comes to mind, and if weren't so serious, it could be viewed as quite comical.

We had laced up to Gorton's schooner *Pollyanna* at the breakwater. The coast guard had towed her from the banks. We proceeded into the harbor and everything was going along fine. Orders were to dock at Slade Gorton's in East Gloucester.

The *Pollyanna*, built in Essex for Gorton Pew in 1915, was only 97 feet long, but was 119 gross tons. She was in her own right a heavy vessel, and coupled with a good load of fish, she had to be handled with some care. The engineer of the vessel had nothing to do, so he came over to watch how the tug's engine worked. Well, the boss rang me down, and we coasted for a ways.

Now the bell system for tugs, and for most other engine rooms, is simple enough. When secured to the wharf and the engine is stopped, a "jingle" means either get ready for maneuvering or "through with the engine"—from stop to slow ahead (one bell); normal ahead (one jingle); wide open (as many jingles as the boss can ring up). To go astern from a standing stop, it's two bells for slow astern; one jingle for normal astern; wide open was much as the bag of bolts can muster.

The word "bell" is a misnomer. The instrument is actually dish-shaped and is called a gong. It is made to sound by the means of a spring-loaded hammer. On the other hand, the "jingle" is similar to a dinner bell rung at the table. The different bells are used to eliminate any confusion in the sounds and the message intended.

In some modern engine rooms, a telegraph is used. This instrument is actuated in the wheelhouse, and it transmits by wires instructions to a similar one that is located at the operator's station in the engine room. The engineer answers the captain's instructions by repeating the printed message on the wheelhouse instrument. That way, there is a positive message for both parties to see.

The bell in the *Mariner's* engine room worked like a trip hammer; that is, the captain pulled up on the grip in the wheelhouse somewhat, and let go; or he raised the hammer all the way, and the hammer would strike the gong. The hammer was spring loaded, and it would register on the gong.

Along about abreast of the old coast guard base 7, the captain gave the double bells to stop engine. We could coast along for the rest of the way. We were getting close to the Slade Gorton dock, so he gave me the bells (so he thought) to go astern. Trouble was he didn't let the tripper go for the second bell to sound. I cannot second-guess what's going on topside, nor should I assume to do so. With only one gong registering, I dutifully went slow ahead. He must have realized that we were not slowing down, so he rung me up, wide open.

Now we were picking up a little speed and it then must have dawned on him what was happening. Quick as a wink, the bells were sounding like a Chinese fire drill. I gave it everything it had in reverse and the nose of the vessel came to a stop within inches of the wharf.

Next thing I heard was "Don't you know the *blankaty-blank* bells yet?" That sort of thing (I cleaned up the language a bit). When he got through chewing me out, and before he had left, I asked the engineer of the *Pollyanna*, who was standing there, what the bells were. He looked the old man right in the eye and said that the chief answered the bells correctly. Dad turned on his heel and with that I heard no more about it.

But I had learned a valuable lesson also. I watched the hammer as well as listen to the gong, and many times after that episode, I did anticipate what he wanted when I saw the hammer come down but not ring it up.

THE *MOTHER ANN*

Which brings to mind another tale. The date was April 3, 1947. The *Mariner* was to go to Essex and bring Gorton's new vessel the *Mother Ann* to Gloucester after her launch. We were short handed, so brother Bill was pressed into service as deckhand. Like any "new" hand, he was unaware of where to stand during operations so as not to get in an untenable and dangerous position.

The *Mother Ann* was one of the deepest draft vessels of the time, 12.5 feet, and 105.5 feet in length. The channel was somewhat filled in with sand bars here and there, and

The tug *Mariner* towing the *Mother Ann* on the Annisquam River, 1947. *Master Mariners Yearbook.*

on the way out, under a short towline, she fetched up on a bar. The captain had me reverse the engine, so as to lay alongside, and without shifting the towing hawser, ease her off the bar.

In doing so, the hawser would lead forward from the after bitts. Bill, taking in the slack of the line and not aware of the position he had taken, let his foot get trapped in a bite of the line. I heard some yelling, and having worked on deck for some time, had an idea of what was happening.

Without any order to do so, I went "full ahead" to stop any movement of the tug, and went topside to see what was the matter. I had guessed right. If Bill had been "trapped" between the after bitts and the deckhouse, he surely would have ended up with some broken bones. As it was, he lost some skin on his legs, but otherwise he was okay. That was the first and the last time Bill volunteered for deck service.

This edition must have an end. Much more of the everyday trials and tribulations could be set down in this synopsis, but most of it could be considered boring. It is enough to say that this, then, is a long overdue accounting of a part of the waterfront's widely varying scenes of activity dealing with the steamboats and the various other crafts that made this port great. In writing this piece, it is my hope that the elder reader enjoys with me recalling the times of years gone by, and for the younger set, a vision of times when life was set at a more leisurely pace.

A SHORT POSTSCRIPT

7

THE *SAWDUST SALLY*

My friend Joe Garland said a history of the Gloucester steamboats would not be complete without the tale of my small steamboat, the *Sawdust Sally*. I had thought about having a small steamer ever since my experiences on the steam tug *Eveleth* back in 1935–1936. I'll make this as short as possible.

It has its beginnings in May of 1963, at the far end of Smith's Cove in East Gloucester. I found a 26-foot Monomy pulling boat, a double-ender at that. I bought it for $25. My wife thought I was crazy, but I figured that it would raise an eyebrow or two around the waterfront.

I brought it over to my house, and with some ingenuity, put a shaft log in it; some people thought I couldn't do it. I had a one-cylinder steam engine for a long time, about 1 $7/16$ horsepower (tongue in cheek), just right for this hull. My friend, the late Russell Grinnell, had an upright boiler that he used to steam some frames and planks for his new vessel. He had no further use for the boiler and gave it to me as a gift.

Moving along a couple of months, the basics were installed: engine, boiler, hot well and pump, oil tank for fuel, etc. I filled the boiler to the top with water, and tested the boiler at 225 pounds for two hours. No leaks. Operating pressure to be used, about 100 pounds. All O.K.

To get steam up, I rigged a spray nozzle combining fuel oil and a small tank of "country" gas. It worked out fine, got up about 15 pounds of steam, then I let the steam alone atomize the oil. The boiler's firebrick was then hot enough to sustain the fire.

For four years, sometimes a couple times a week, I tooled around the harbor and up the nearby Annisquam River. I had a lot of fun, but after a while, it got too much for me, and

Sawdust Sally, now owned by "Knobby" Lasley. *J.L. Sutherland.*

Sawdust Sally at first light in 1963. *J.L. Sutherland.*

Sawdust Sally four years later on the New Hampshire lakes. *J.L. Sutherland.*

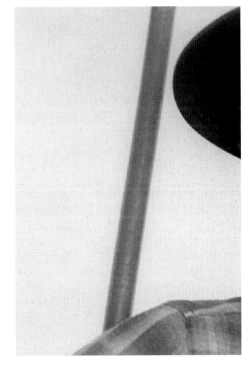

John Sutherland on *Sawdust Sally* on the Annisquam River. *J.L. Sutherland.*

I sold her to a person on the lakes of New Hampshire. As far as I know, she's still steaming away.

Now, I did not want to write about this, it sounds like too much bragging, but Joe, resident historian, said I had to—he said it would fit right in.

One day, while steaming along the shore of Niles's Beach, I came up to Black Bess, a rock outcropping offshore near Joe's house. I was moving right along, at a pretty good clip, (about five knots). I gave him a long blast on the whistle. He still talks about it whenever he can get an ear.

So much for this yarn, except that it must be said, in all modesty, that I was captain, crew, and engineer of the last working steamboat operating in Gloucester Harbor. Also, my wife, Natalie, was the first mate, on the boat, as well as in marriage.

EPILOGUE

At this time, it has to be said that I was not old enough to have lived in most of the early days just described, having come into this world in 1922. My own observations and referrals about the steamboats *Cape Ann* and the *City of Gloucester* came to me as a member of the household that had in it a person who did live those days as an oiler and assistant engineer on the *Cape Ann*. That person was my dad.

In 1917, when the *Cape Ann* was sold, he shifted over as the assistant engineer on the *City of Gloucester*, working under Chief Bumpus's license. On November 4, 1920, with his years of experience on the *Cape Ann* and *City of Gloucester*, my dad sat for his engineer's license in the customhouse in Boston, and received a test score of 92 percent. He then became the legally qualified assistant engineer on the *City*. In about 1924–25, he transferred as engineer on the towboat *Eveleth*, a position he held as stockholder and chief until 1937, when the *Eveleth* was sold. Dad was engineer on the diesel tug *Mariner* until 1945, and when Captain Loren Jacobs passed away, he took the position of captain. When I came home from the service, I filled in as the engineer. This was the setup until 1947, when the *Mariner* was sold. Thus, commercial towing came to an end. After my father acquired his stationary steam license, he secured a position at Burnham's railway as fireman and steam engineer for a few years until he finally retired.

My own experiences on the tugs *Eveleth* and *Mariner* are set down as I remember them. My only regret is that I did not have the "smarts" when my father was with me to get more of his firsthand views on tape, for I know there was more—much more—to tell.

I leaned somewhat on the observations of the late Gordon W. Thomas, a name well known in Gloucester and a historian of some note. His article in the *Gloucester Daily Times* of June 14, 1952, inspired me to detail some of the finer points of his article. In the years that have since past, the article jogged the memories and tales related by my father; the result may be of some use to the history buffs of today and those to follow.

I also want to thank Dana A. Story, son of the famous shipwright Arthur D. Story of Essex, and a shipwright as well, for his photos of the *Eveleth* at a few of the early launchings. His publication *The Ship Builders of Essex* is one of my "must" volumes. I observed many of the Essex launchings in the thirties and forties, first as a youngster on the *Eveleth*, and later on the *Mariner*.

And last, but not in the least, I would like to acknowledge Joseph E. Garland, resident author and historian of Gloucester, with his many publications, including *Gloucester on the Wind* with the general information on the harbor and tugs.

As a member in good standing in the University of Baltimore Library and the Steamship Historical Society, Inc., I am indebted for the photos of the steamer *Cape Ann, City of Gloucester*, and *Rio Branco*.

The broadside photo of the *Cape Ann* (seen on page 55) from the collection of "Patt" was instrumental in my building the model of this vessel now on display in the Sawyer Free Library in Gloucester.

A model of the S.S. *Cape Ann*, built by John L. Sutherland in 1998. *J.L. Sutherland.*

A postcard of S.S. *Cape Ann*, *c.* 1900. *J.L. Sutherland.*

APPENDICES

THE NORTH SHORE STEAMBOATS
1847—1931

SIDE-WHEEL TYPE STEAMBOATS

Jacob Bell: tonnage: 229.83; measurement: 141.2 x 21 x 8; built 1842, New York

Yacht: tonnage: 249.64; measurement: 140 x 22.5 x 8.3; built 1844, New York

Mystic: tonnage: 154.00; measurement: 117.3 x 21 x 6.7; built 1852, New London, Connecticut
   (U.S. transport during the Civil War; lost 1865)

Emeline: official number 7225; tonnage: 274.26; measurement: 162.5 x 25.8 x 8.1; built 1857, New York
   (ex-*Nantasket*; tonnage: 285.89 when built)

Escort: official number 7972; tonnage: 675.15; measurement: 185 x 28 x. 9.6; built 1862, Mystic,
   Connecticut (later *Catskill* and *City of Hudson*; tonnage: 453.31 when built)

Ulysses: built in Boston, 1863, for the Boston to Nahant Route

Charles Houghton: official number 4253; tonnage: 268.67; measurement: 131.1 x 32.4 x 9.0;
   built 1863, Boston, Massachusetts

Nathaniel P. Banks: official number 18506; tonnage: 399.55; measurement: 167.4 x 27.6 x 19.1;
   built 1863, Boston, Massachusetts

Stamford: official number 22430; tonnage: 284.54; measurement: 168.8 x 28.1 x 8.2; built 1863,
   Brooklyn, New York (later *John Endicott*)

Regulator: official number: 21548; tonnage: 318.80; measurement: 153.6 x 26.8 x 8.1; built 1864,
   Portland, Maine (436.75 tons as shown in 1866)

W.W. Coit; official number 26775; tonnage: 484.72; measurement: 172.72 x 26 x 9; built 1864,
   Mystic, Connecticut (measurement: 399.29 x 173.3 x 36 x 9.2 when built)

Admiral: official number unknown; tonnage: 1,248.50; measurement: 220 x 34.5 x 7.2; built Fairhaven,
   Connecticut (later S.S. *Fort Morgan* and S.S. *Cuba*)

Mischief: Information unavailable

Fanny: Information unavailable

Three Brothers: tonnage: 357.25; other information unavailable

PROPELLER-DRIVEN STEAMBOATS

Ellie Knight: official number 7062; tonnage: 389.78; measurement: 151 x 23.3 x 7;
   built 1863, Philadelphia, Pennsylvania
George A. Chaffee: official number 75095; tonnage: 293.34; measurement: 108 x 26 x 7.5;
   built 1870, Middletown, Connecticut (later *Jetty*)
City of Gloucester: official number 126139; tonnage: 561.00; measurement: 192 x 28 x 11.6;
   built 1883, Brooklyn, New York (later *Thames*)
Mascotte: official number 91818; tonnage: 884; measurement: 207 x 30 x 19.6;
   built 1885, Philadelphia, Pennsylvania
Cape Ann: official number 127074; tonnage: 719; measurement: 185 x 28 x 13.5; built 1895,
   Philadelphia, Pennsylvania (later *Seminole* [French])
City of Haverhill: official number 127661; tonnage: 343; measurement: 121.7 x 24 x 10.7; built 1902,
   Boston, Massachusetts (later *Mildred*)
Monhegan: official number 93395; tonnage: 367; measurement: 126 x 26.7 x 11.2;
   built 1903, Rockland, Maine
Governor Prence: official number 224952; tonnage: 83; measurement: 104.3 x 15 x 8.1;
   built 1917, Kingston, New York (ex-U.S.N. SC-85)
Roseway: official number 217121; tonnage: 479; measurement: 142.1 x 29.6 x 11.8;
   built 1918, Essex, Massachusetts (steam trawler) (later motor vessel)
Myrtle II: official number 130934; tonnage: 503; measurement: 151.9 x 28.1 x 11.8;
   built Boston, Massachusetts (ex-*New Shoreham*)
J.M. Todd: tonnage: 94.35; other information unavailable

THE OFFICERS, CREWS
AND GENERAL EMPLOYEES

In the early days of towboating, ledgers and records must have been kept to account for the everyday profits and losses of the various concerns. Over the past 127 years, only the books of the Master Mariners' Towboat Co., dating from 1924 to 1947, have been preserved. Perhaps lying buried in a trunk in some dusty attic, there are other records that will eventually surface. The records provide not only a glimpse into how these companies operated, but also who their employees were.

There is another aspect of activity within the confines of the harbor that is in need of recognition. Little has been written about the small workhorses that shepherded the fishing vessels in, out, and around the harbor. From the mid-1800s to the mid-1940s, Gloucester tugs and other smaller craft had contributed much to the prosperity of this city. It is close to 50 years since the last commercial tugs left this port for good. To scan the shelves at our library, it reveals, in many respects, that the primary purpose and focus of the numerous authors is upon the great fishing fleet that sailed the waters of the North Atlantic.

There is no question that the vessel builders and the men that labored in their various trades deserve the lion's share of recognition. No occupation was, nor is, by comparison more fraught with dangers that imperiled lives on a daily basis. The many supporting craft that prowled the harbor provided a vital service to the fleet and they have only been mentioned perhaps to add a bit of color, as it were, to fill a page or two in some book.

All of the small craft—the tugs, the water boats, and the ferryboats—have long since vanished, along with most of the crews that manned them. With them has gone what I consider an important phase, though not as stimulating a phase of our history as the fishing vessels that spread their white wings and regrettably sailed into oblivion.

The resulting effort forthcoming is due in a large part to painstaking page-by-page research through the Sawyer Library's volumes of the city of Gloucester directories. These volumes contain the names of most of the citizens of Gloucester, their occupations and residences. A methodical review of the data revealed that most of the professional occupations that could be aligned to towboating are stated as "engineer" or "captain of a tow-boat." "Engineer" could well mean a stationary engineer working in a quarry or on a fishing vessel. "Captain of a towboat" narrows it down somewhat, but does nothing to bring to light the individual's particular tug. Living relatives of men who plied their trades a hundred or more years ago on tugs are almost impossible to find. Many phone calls have been made, few produced results.

At least what is recorded here will give some indication that the towboat industry and other related harbor craft have earned a place in history along with the fishing vessels of the port of Gloucester.

STEAM TUGS

Eveleth: built in 1897 at Bishop's yard in Vincent's Cove for the Gloucester Towboat Co. Named after Dr. Edward Eveleth (1842–1916), surgeon and physician who had his office and residence at 20 Highland Street, East Gloucester. Crew: Captain Charles T. Heberle (1899–1900), resided at 8 Summit Street, Gloucester (later at 6 Commonwealth Avenue); Captain Osborn P. "Obie" Linnekin (1901), resided at 12 Lookout Street, Gloucester; Captain Andrew E. Jacobs (1901–1931), resided at 10 Essex Avenue and 5 Prospect Square, Gloucester; Mate John E. Holley (1902–1903), resided at 92 Eastern Avenue, Gloucester; Mate Loren A. Jacobs, later captain (1931–1937), resided at Pine Street; Mate William Helme Jacobs (1931–1937), Rockport; Engineer Israel K. Crosby (1903–1911), resided at 9 Pew Court; Engineer William J. Sutherland (1924–1937), resided at 86 East Main Street; Fireman Morrell "Honk" Jacobs, Arlington; Fireman Albert "Al" Caston, resided at 4½ Perkins Street; Fireman Roy "Hoss" Sutherland, resided at 86 East Main Street. In 1937, the *Eveleth* was sold to John Forward of the John Forward Contracting Co., Providence, Rhode Island. It was converted to diesel at that time. Last I heard, it burned to the water's edge and sank in New York and was raised and rebuilt. Its whereabouts after that are unknown.

Joe Call: built in 1882 by Arthur D. Story in Essex. Named for a local spar maker (whose yard was located up in the far reaches of the then-Vincent's Cove); sold to interests in Portland, Maine, in 1911. Crew: Captain Henry Smith (1886); Captain Walter Smith (1896–1902); Mate Andrew Smith (1902–1903); Engineer Samuel E. Smith (1902).

Little Charlie: Named after captain's son, Charles Jr. Crew: Captain Charles T. Heberle (1896–1899). Heberle's own tug was bought secondhand in New York. The *Charlie* sank twice. The second time, it was laid up as a derelict in the far reaches of Smith Cove, East Gloucester.

Mariner: built June 6, 1907, for the Gloucester Towboat Co. by Tarr and James in Essex. Crew: Captain Andrew R. Smith (1907–1911), resided at 27 Wonson Street, Gloucester; Captain Loren A. Jacobs (1937–1944), re-sided on Pine Street, Gloucester; Captain William J. Sutherland (1944–1947), resided at 86 East Main Street, Gloucester; Fireman Samuel Smith (pre-1930), resided at 4 Hammond Street; Engineer William J. Sutherland (1937–1944), resided at 86 East Main Street, Gloucester; Engineer John L. Sutherland (1945–1947), resided at 86 East Main Street, Gloucester. In 1937, the *Mariner* was converted to diesel and sold in 1947 by the Master Mariners' Towboat Co. to Russell Towboat Co. of New York.

Nellie: built June 1902, by Arthur D. Story for the Gloucester Towboat Co. Crew: Captain Osborn P. Linnekin (1905–1911), resided at 12 Lookout Street, Gloucester; Engineer Charles E. Locke (1913), resided at 5 Oak Street, Gloucester; Mate Peter J. Saxild (1913), later engineer (1916), resided at 10 Decatur Street, Gloucester.

The *Nellie* was probably sold in the teens to Boston interests, perhaps the Bay State Dredge and Dock Co., and renamed the *Gorham H. Whitney.*

Priscilla: built by Arthur D. Story in Essex for the Gloucester Towboat Co. and launched on April 8, 1901. Crew: Captain Charles Heberle (1901–1903), resided at 6 Comm. Avenue, Gloucester; Mate Nathan L. Smith (1903), resided at 136 East Main Street, Gloucester; Engineer Edward Ashley (1902–1903), resided at 76 Parker Street, Gloucester.

Startle: built in 1889 either by Bishop or Poland and Woodburg in Vincent's Cove. Crew: Captain Osborn "Obie" Linnekin (1889–1901), resided 12 Lookout Street, Gloucester.

Towboats listed in the years 1899–1900 directory were *Eveleth* (Captain Charles T. Heberle), *Joe Call* (Captain Walter Smith), and *Startle* (Captain Osborn "Obie" Linnekin).

Towboats listed in the year 1902 directory were *Eveleth* (Captain Andrew E. Jacobs), *Joe Call* (Captain Walter Smith), *Priscilla* (Captain Heberle), and *Nellie* (Captain Linnekin). Why other towboats like the *Startle* were not listed is a matter of conjecture.

In November 1925, the Gloucester Towboat Co. ceased to exist and became the Master Mariners' Towboat Co., with only two tugs: the *Eveleth* and the *Mariner.*

SOME OTHER STEAM VESSELS

Not all of the steam-powered vessels of Gloucester and their crews are named here. A few were here only a short time before transferring to other ports. Not all the vessels were workboats, as in the case of the *Alice M. Jacobs*, which was built by A.D. Story in Essex and launched on March 11, 1902. As a mackerel seiner, she had the lines of a rather long towboat (141 feet). She was steam powered with a compound 300-horsepower engine. In 1903, she was wrecked on the shores of Newfoundland.

STEAM POWER

Little Giant: ferryboat; built 1878 by Poland & Woodburg. Crew: Captain John C. Foster (1911), resided at 259 East Main Street, Gloucester; Captain Augustus F. Cunningham (1913–1915), resided at 61 Washington Street, Gloucester; Engineers Addison Lowe and John C. Foster.

Eben Hodge: steam tug; built around 1889 by Moses Adams.

Moses Adams: steam lighter; built 1885 by Moses Adams in Essex.

Eagle: steam lighter; built in 1887 in Gloucester by A.D. Story for Tom Reed. The *Eagle* was blown up with dynamite, burned, and then sank at Salt Island for a movie (the serial *Black Beard, the Pirate*, episode 13). Tom Reed also donated an old schooner, which was also destroyed at the same time.

William H. Moody: steam lighter; built in 1898 by A.D. Story. The *Moody* was instrumental in building the Rockport breakwater.

Ego: steam lighter. Crew: Captain Alfred W. Spurr (1902), resided on Gerring Road.

Abbott Coffin: steam lighter, built 1904. Crew: James M. Carrigan, resided at 5 Allen Street, Gloucester; Engineer Albert P. Ames, resided at 14 Chestnut Street, Gloucester.

Philip: steam lighter, built 1906, perhaps at Bishop's Yard. Crew: Captain Alfred W. Spurr (1917), resided on Gerring Road; Captain Salvatore Santapola; Engineer Daniel W. Wiley (1902); Mate Joseph Santapola; *Mate Salvatore Puglisi*; Engineer Daniel W. Wiley.

Around 1886, there were four other tugs that serviced the harbor: *Vim, Camilla, Emma S. Bradford* (Captain Eli O. Cleaves), and the *Sarah E. Witherell* (Captain Osborn Linnekin).

SAIL AND MOTOR POWER

There were a few water boats that serviced the vessels with "fresh" potable water. I say "fresh," but that depended a great deal on how often the cypress tanks were cleaned out.

Aqua Pura: sloop; built in Essex; measurement: 39 feet. Crew: Captain Eli O. Cleaves (1902), resided at 7 Marchant Street.
Maggie Cannon: sloop; built in Essex; measurement: 30 feet.
Puritan: sloop; built in Essex; measurement: 31 feet.
Lillian Russell: sloop; built in Essex; measurement: 35 feet.
Undine: sloop; built in Essex; measurement: 32 feet.
Wenham Lake: probably built in Gloucester; measurement: 35 feet. Crew: Captains John E. and Herbert Wennerberg. Like the early water boats, *Wenham Lake* was first a sloop and then later powered by a Lathrop gas engine. It proved to be the last water boat in Gloucester.
Wanderrer: water boat; built 1881 in Gloucester probably by Thomas Irving.

It is unknown if all these water boats worked Gloucester Harbor, most did. Some of the men that worked these boats are listed below.

John C. Foster, harbormaster, literage and water boat; resided at 259 East Main Street.

John Healy, water boatman; resided at 12 Smith Street.

Allen McDonald, water boatman; resided at 20 Locust Street.

THE BOSTON AND GLOUCESTER
STEAMSHIP COMPANY
1859—1926

The officers and crew of the *Cape Ann* on her maiden voyage from Philadelphia on June 5, 1895:
    Captain: Henry M. Godfrey, 1895–1917 (of Lubec, Maine)
    Pilot: George Bearse (of Boston, Massachusetts)
    First Mate: Leo Campbell (of Boston, Massachusetts)
    Chief Engineer: Frank Fowles, 1895–1902 (of Gloucester)
    Assistant Engineer: Frank Daniels (of Somerville, Massachusetts)
    Steward: Herbert Lane (Everett, Massachusetts)

Cape Ann Officers and Crew 1902–1917
    Captain: Henry M. Godfrey 1895-1917
    Pilot: George Bearse 1885–1910
    First Mate: Leo Campbell, resided at 43 Warner Street, Gloucester
    Second Mate: Warren Fowles, resided at 23 Chestnut Street, Gloucester
    Mate: John I. Ivester
    Chief Engineer: Frank Fowles, resided at 23 Chestnut Street, Gloucester (formerly 23 School Street)
    Chief Engineer: Eugene Connolly 1909–1917 (of East Boston)
    Assistant Engineer: Herbert Sullivan
    Oiler: William J. Sutherland 1910–1917, resided at 86 East Main Street, Gloucester

George A. Chaffee (later *Jetty*) Officers and Crew 1863–1883 (sold in 1895)
    Captain: E.S. Young
    Captain: Nehemia Proctor

City of Gloucester (later *Thames*) Officers and Crew 1883–1902
    Captain: E.S. Young
    Captain: Nehemiah Proctor

1902–1915
    Captain: Osborne Linnekin, resided at 12 Lookout Street
    Captain: Albert Ober (of Somerville, Massachusetts)
    Pilot: George Bacon, 1902–1911 (of Boson, Massachusetts)
    Pilot: George Bearse, 1911–1915
    First Mate: George Means (of Chelsea, Massachusetts)
    Mate: Leo Campbell, 1884–1885, resided at 43 Warner Street, Gloucester
    Chief Engineer: Nathaniel Frost, 1911 (of Malden, Massachusetts)
    Assistant Engineer: Frank Daniels
    First Assistant Engineer: Albert P. Ames, resided at 14 Chestnut Street, Gloucester (in 1902, he was an engineer on the lighter *Abbott Coffin*)

1917–1926
    Captain and Master: "Hans" Larson, 1923–1926
    Chief Engineer: Charles W. Bumpus, 1917–1926
    Mate: Loren A. Jacobs, 1926
    First Assistant Engineer: William J. Sutherland, 1920–1923
    Agent: Edward Carpenter, 1925–1926 (also the agent for the steamship *Mascotte*)

Some of the dates of employment may seem confusing, only because the officers moved around from vessel to vessel trying to improve their lot. Listed below are some of the office help and other employees that toiled for the company over the years.

    Clerk: Harry Barber
    Clerk: Lester Brown
    Clerk: Leonard Dodge
    Clerk: John J. McEachern, resided at 67 Pleasant Street
    Clerk: William McCormack
    Freight Handler: C. Warren McCormack
    Freight Handler: Stanford J. Munroe
    Freight Handler: Arthur O'Neill
    Freight Handler: Ernest Saunders
    Freight Handler: Arthur C. Tarr
    Freight Handler: Edward Todd
    Head Bookkeeper: Stephen Dodge, resided at 70 Centennial Avenue, Gloucester
    Steward: Fred Wagner (of Chelsea, Massachusetts)
    Watchman: Louis C. Johnson
    Watchman: Manual F. Machado, resided at 31 Taylor Street
    Watchman: Manual Marshall

On the last trip of the *City of Gloucester* to Fort Point Channel in South Boston near the Congress Street Bridge, the officers were as follows:

    Captain: Fred H. Pray
    Mate: Loren A. Jacobs
    Chief Engineer: Charles W. Bumpus

From time to time, many men and women had positions with the company, but because of incomplete records, most names are untraceable.